♈   THE ARIES ENIGMA   ♈

Cracking the Code

ALSO BY JANE RIDDER-PATRICK

A Handbook of Medical Astrology
Shaping Your Future (Series of 12 titles)
Shaping Your Relationships (Series of 12 titles)

The Zodiac Code series

THE

ARIES

ENIGMA

Cracking the Code

JANE RIDDER-PATRICK

MAINSTREAM
PUBLISHING

EDINBURGH AND LONDON

For Katie Wood whose spontaneous generosity
and do-it-now Aries energy set this series in motion

First published in Great Britain in 2004 by
MAINSTREAM PUBLISHING COMPANY
(EDINBURGH) LTD
7 Albany Street
Edinburgh EH1 3UG

ISBN 1 84018 535 X

A catalogue record for this book is available
from the British Library

Typeset in Allise and Van Dijck

Printed in Great Britain by
Cox & Wyman Ltd

Contents

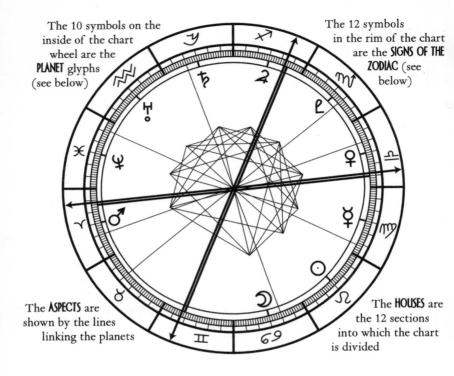

The 10 symbols on the inside of the chart wheel are the **PLANET** glyphs (see below)

The 12 symbols in the rim of the chart are the **SIGNS OF THE ZODIAC** (see below)

The **ASPECTS** are shown by the lines linking the planets

The **HOUSES** are the 12 sections into which the chart is divided

A Sample Birth Chart

Sign	Ruler	Sign	Ruler
Aries ♈	Mars ♂	Libra ♎	Venus ♀
Taurus ♉	Venus ♀	Scorpio ♏	Pluto ♇
Gemini ♊	Mercury ☿	Sagittarius ♐	Jupiter ♃
Cancer ♋	Moon ☽	Capricorn ♑	Saturn ♄
Leo ♌	Sun ☉	Aquarius ♒	Uranus ♅
Virgo ♍	Mercury ☿	Pisces ♓	Neptune ♆

ONE

The Truth of Astrology

MOST PEOPLE'S FIRST EXPERIENCE OF ASTROLOGY IS THROUGH newspapers and magazines. This is a mixed blessing for astrology's reputation – writing an astrology column to any degree of accuracy is a tough, many would say impossible, challenge. The astrologer has to try to say something meaningful about conditions that affect every single person belonging to the same sign, over a very short period of time, in a scant handful of words. The miracle is that some talented astrologers do manage to get across a tantalising whiff of the real thing and keep readers coming back for more of what most of us are hungry for – self-knowledge and reassurance about the future. The downside of the popularity of these columns is that many people think that all astrology is a branch of the entertainment industry and is limited to light-hearted fortune-telling. This is far from the truth.

What Astrology Can Offer
Serious astrology is one of the most sophisticated tools available to help us understand ourselves and the world

around us. It gives us a language and a framework to examine and describe – quite literally – *anything* under the Sun, from countries to companies, from money markets to medical matters. Its most common application, however, is in helping people to understand themselves better using their own unique birth charts. Astrology has two main functions. One is to describe the traits and tendencies of whatever system is being examined, whether this is a state, a software company or someone's psyche. The other is to give an astonishingly accurate timetable for important changes within that entity. In the chapters that follow, we'll be using astrology to investigate the psychology of the innermost part of your personality, taking a look at what drives, inspires and motivates you.

Astrology uses an ancient system of symbols to describe profound truths about the nature of life on earth, truths that cannot be weighed and measured, but ones we recognise nevertheless, and that touch and move us at a deep level. By linking mythology and mathematics, astrology bridges the gap between our inner lives and our outer experiences, between mind and matter, between poetry and science.

Fate and Free Will

Some people think that astrology is all about foretelling the future, the implication being that everything is predestined and that we have no say in how our lives take shape. None of that is true. We are far from being helpless victims of fate. Everything that happens to us at any given time is the result of past choices. These choices may have been our own, or made by other people. They could even have been made long ago before we, or even our grandparents, were born. It is not always possible to prevent processes that were set in motion in the past from coming to their logical conclusions as events that we then have to deal with. We are, however, all free to decide how to react to whatever is presented to us at every moment of our lives.

Your destiny is linked directly with your personality because the choices you make, consciously or unconsciously, depend largely on your own natural inclinations. It is these inclinations that psychological astrology describes. You can live out every single part of your chart in a constructive or a less constructive way. For instance, if you have Aries strong in your chart, action and initiative will play a major role in your life. It is your choice whether you express yourself aggressively or assertively, heroically or selfishly, and also whether you are the doer or the done-to. Making the right choices is important because every decision has consequences – and what you give out, sooner or later, you get back. If you don't know and understand yourself, you are 'fated' to act according to instinct and how your life experiences have conditioned you. By revealing how you are wired up temperamentally, astrology can highlight alternatives to blind knee-jerk reactions, which often make existing problems worse. This self-knowledge can allow you to make more informed free-will choices, and so help you create a better and more successful future for yourself.

Astrology and Prediction

Astrology cannot predict specific events based on your birth chart. That kind of prediction belongs to clairvoyance and divination. These specialities, when practised by gifted and responsible individuals, can give penetrating insights into events that are likely to happen in the future if matters proceed along their present course.

The real benefit of seeing into the future is that if we don't like what could happen if we carry on the way we're going, we can take steps either to prevent it or to lessen its impact. Rarely is the future chiselled out in stone. There are many possible futures. What you feed with your attention grows. Using your birth chart, a competent astrologer can map out, for years in advance, major turning points, showing which areas of your life will be affected at these times and the kind of change that will be taking place. This information gives answers to the questions that most clients ask in one way or another: 'Why me, why this and why now?' If you accept responsibility for facing what needs to be done at the appropriate time, and doing it, you can change the course of your life for the better.

Astrology and the Soul

What is sometimes called the soul and its purpose is a mystery much more profound than astrology. Most of us have experienced 'chance' meetings and apparent 'tragedies' which have affected the direction of our entire lives. There is an intelligence at work that is infinitely wiser and more powerful than the will or wishes of our small egocentric personalities. This force, whatever name we give it – Universal Wisdom, the Inner Guide, the Self, a guardian angel – steers us into exactly the right conditions for our souls' growth. Astrology can pinpoint the turning points in the course of your destiny and describe the equipment that you have at your disposal for serving, or resisting, the soul's purpose. That equipment is your personality.

Who Are You?

You are no doubt aware of your many good qualities as well as your rather more resistible ones that you might prefer to keep firmly under wraps. Maybe you have wondered why it is that one part of your personality seems to want to do one thing while another part is stubbornly intent on doing the exact opposite. Have you ever wished that you could crack the code that holds the secrets of what makes you – and significant others – behave in the complex way you do? The good news is that you can, with the help of your astrological birth chart, sometimes known as your horoscope.

Just as surely as your DNA identifies you and distinguishes you from everyone else, as well as encoding your peculiarities and potential, your birth chart reveals the unique 'DNA fingerprinting' of your personality. This may seem a staggering claim, but it is one that those who have experienced serious astrology will endorse, so let's take a closer look at what a birth chart is.

Your Birth Chart

Your birth chart is a simplified diagram of the positions of the planets, as seen from the place of your birth, at the moment you took your first independent breath. Critics have said that astrology is obviously nonsense because birth charts are drawn up as if the Sun and all the planets moved round the Earth.

We know in our minds that the Earth moves round the Sun, but that doesn't stop us seeing the Sun rise in the east in the morning and move across the sky to set in the west in the evening. This is an optical illusion. In the same way, we know (or at least most of us know) that we are not really the centre of the universe, but that doesn't stop us experiencing ourselves as being at the focal point of our own personal worlds. It is impossible to live life in any other way. It is the strength, not weakness, of astrology that it describes from your own unique viewpoint how you, as an individual, experience life.

Erecting Your Chart

To draw up a full birth chart you need three pieces of information – the date, time and place of your birth. With your birth date alone you can find the positions of all the planets (except sometimes the Moon) to a good enough degree of accuracy to reveal a great deal of important information about you. If you have the time and place of birth, too, an astrologer can calculate your Ascendant or Rising Sign and the houses of your chart – see below. The Ascendant is a bit like the front door of your personality and describes your general outlook on life. (If you know your Ascendant sign, you might like to read more about its characteristics in the book on that sign in this series.)

The diagram on page 6 shows what a birth chart looks like. Most people find it pretty daunting at first sight but it actually breaks down into only four basic units – the planets, the signs, the aspects and the houses.

The Planets

Below is a simple list of what the planets represent.

PLANET	REPRESENTS YOUR URGE TO
☉ The Sun	express your identity
☽ The Moon	feel nurtured and safe
☿ Mercury	make connections
♀ Venus	attract what you love
♂ Mars	assert your will
♃ Jupiter	find meaning in life
♄ Saturn	achieve your ambitions
♅ Uranus	challenge tradition
♆ Neptune	serve an ideal
♇ Pluto	eliminate, transform and survive

The planets represent the main psychological drives that we all share. The exact way in which we express these drives is not fixed from birth but develops and evolves throughout our lives, both consciously and unconsciously. In this book we will be examining in detail four of these planets – your Sun, Moon, Mercury and Venus. These are the bodies that are right at the heart of our solar system. They correspond, in psychological astrology, to the core of your personality and represent how you express yourself, what motivates you emotionally, how you use your mind and what brings you pleasure.

The Signs
The signs your planets are in show how you tend to express your inner drives. For example, if your Mars is in the action sign of Aries, you will assert yourself pretty directly, pulling no punches. If your Venus is in secretive Scorpio, you will attract, and also be attracted to, emotionally intense relationships. There is a summary of all of the signs on p. 128.

The Aspects
Aspects are important relationships between planets and whether your inner characteristics clash with or complement each other depends largely on whether or not they are in aspect and whether that aspect is an easy or a challenging one. In Chapter Six we'll be looking at some challenging aspects to the Sun.

The Houses
Your birth chart is divided into 12 slices, called houses, each of which is associated with a particular area of life, such as friendships, travel or home life. If, for example, you have your Uranus in the house of career, you are almost

certainly a bit of a maverick at work. If you have your Neptune in the house of partnership, you are likely to idealise your husband, wife or business partner.

The Nature of Time

Your birth chart records a moment in time and space, like a still from a movie – the movie being the apparent movement of the planets round the earth. We all know that time is something that can be measured in precise units, which are always the same, like seconds, months and centuries. But if you stop to reflect for a moment, you'll also recognise that time doesn't always feel the same. Twenty minutes waiting for a bus on a cold, rainy day can seem like a miserable eternity, while the same amount of time spent with someone you love can pass in a flash. As Einstein would say – that's relativity.

There are times in history when something significant seems to be in the air, but even when nothing momentous is happening the quality of time shifts into different 'moods' from moment to moment. Your birth chart is impregnated with the qualities of the time when you were born. For example, people who were born in the mid-to-late 1960s, when society was undergoing major disruptive changes, carry those powerful energies within them and their personalities reflect, in many ways, the turmoil of those troubled and exciting times. Now, as adults, the choices that those individuals make, based on their own inner conflicts and compulsions, will help shape the future of society for better or worse. And so it goes on through the generations.

Seed Meets Soil

There is no such thing as a good or bad chart, nor is any one sign better or worse than another. There are simply 12 different, but equally important, life focuses. It's useful to keep in mind the fact that the chart of each one of us is made up of all the signs of the zodiac. This means that we'll act out, or experience, *every* sign somewhere in our lives. It is true, however, that some individual charts are more challenging than others; but the greater the challenge, the greater the potential for achievement and self-understanding.

In gardening terms, your chart is a bit like the picture on a seed packet. It shows what you could become. If the seeds are of poppies, there's no way you'll get petunias, but external conditions will affect how they grow. With healthy soil, a friendly climate and green-fingered gardeners, the plants have an excellent chance of flourishing. With poor soil, a harsh climate or constant neglect, the seeds will be forced to struggle. This is not always a disadvantage. They can become hardy and adapt, finding new and creative ways of evolving and thriving under more extreme conditions than the plant that was well cared for. It's the same with your chart. The environment you were raised in may have been friendly or hostile to your nature and it will have done much to shape your life until now. Using the insights of astrology to affirm who you are, you can, as an adult, provide your own ideal conditions, become your own best gardener and live out more fully – and successfully – your own highest potential.

TWO

The Symbolism of Aries

WE CAN LEARN A GREAT DEAL ABOUT ARIES BY LOOKING AT the symbolism and the myths and legends associated with it. These are time-honoured ways of describing psychological truths; they carry more information than plain facts alone and hint at the deeper meanings and significance of the sign.

Aries is the sign of the groundbreaker and its symbol, or glyph, looks like a shoot, bursting through from the cold, dark earth into the promise of springtime, fresh, thrusting and ready, like most Ariens, to make its presence felt in a brave new world. Alternatively, the two exuberant strokes of the glyph can be seen as a fountain springing high in the air, depicting the outpouring of life-enhancing energy and unrestrained high spirits found in so many Ariens. It can signify too the eyebrows and nose, which make up the most distinctive features of the face. These stand for individuality and an active brain. Wise Ariens know that their powerful wills must be tempered with a bit of thought. Backed by all that dynamic energy, any Ariens who use their heads usually get ahead, big style.

Most obviously, however, it represents the horns of a ram, highlighting the robust stance of Ariens who are ready and waiting to defend their territory, confront opposition and see any undesirables smartly off their patch. The ram's head mascot was adopted by Greek and Roman soldiers as a symbol of irresistible strength. They used a heavy tree trunk with a ram's head made of iron or bronze at the end of it, called an 'aries' (or 'battering ram'), to smash through the walls or gates of enemy cities. It was said that there was no tower so strong, no wall so thick, that it could resist the force of this machine, if its blows were continued long enough. A bit like you, Aries.

Aries the Ram

The constellation of Aries is associated with the ram whose golden fleece Jason and the Argonauts sailed off to capture. The story is one of the oldest Greek sagas and probably refers to the tough and challenging early exploration of the Black Sea. In order to win back his father's kingdom, Jason had to fetch the golden fleece for his uncle. The fleece was guarded by a ferocious dragon that never slept. As if that wasn't enough, before slaying the dragon he had to carry out some heroic tasks. He had to plough a field with two wild bulls, with hooves of bronze and flaming breath, and then go on to plant it with dragon's teeth. This he did with the help of Medea, a beautiful magician, who fell in love with him. They later married but unfortunately he then blew it by running off with another woman. Medea, in revenge, murdered the children she had by Jason as well as Jason's new lady. Jason's story is a familiar one to many Ariens, whose lives are threaded through with challenge, courage and victory, but can also be disrupted by attack and loss if they get too uppity and ride roughshod over others, especially those who have helped them on their way.

Ruled by Mars

Each sign is associated with a planet, which is called its ruler. The sign has a great deal in common with its ruling planet. Aries is ruled by Mars, who was the Roman god of war. The Greek equivalent of Mars was their own war god, Ares. The contrast between these two gods show how Aries energy can be expressed at best and worst.

Ares was clumsy and uncouth and, with his foul temper, could have benefited from a course in anger management. With his two henchmen Deimos (Fear) and Phobos (Fright), he wasn't a character you would want to rub up the wrong way. When he was crossed, he'd erupt with rage, fists flying. If he wanted something, he'd charge at it and grab, never considering others or giving a thought to the consequences of his actions. As a result, he usually ended up unlucky in love, losing his battles, generally disliked and often a laughing stock.

In contrast, Mars was greatly revered as the god of spring and agriculture as well as of battle. His sons, Romulus and Remus, became the founders of Rome. It was Mars himself who inspired the Romans to go out and conquer the world. His squires, Honos (Honour) and Virtus (Courage), helped instil their virtues into the Roman soldiers. As an Arien, the choice of role model is yours . . .

Aries in Myth and Legend

In fairy tales the supreme power of love is symbolised by the magic sword which can conquer even the most formidable foe, inner as well as outer. Aries is associated with King Arthur and with the Germanic hero, Siegfried. In both cases they received magical swords only they could claim, proving that they had some special heroic destiny to fulfil. Ariens tend to have a sense of their own specialness, but the quality of your life will depend on what this, in the form of your fiery will and energy, serves – your own interests or something higher. If you abuse it, you will lose it. Aries energy works best when it is dedicated, as the knights of old, to honour and to a love higher than self-love.

In the Old Testament a ram, representing the selfishness, arrogance and worldliness of man, was sacrificed on the altar in religious ceremonies. In the New Testament Christ is symbolised by the Lamb of God which takes away the sins of the world through self-sacrifice. Although the symbolism is different, the message is the same as for the magic sword. The will of the personality needs to be purged of purely self-seeking tendencies and be sacrificed – literally, 'be made sacred' – in heroic service in the world.

The Season of Aries

Aries is the sign of the resurrection and beginning of new life and it is no coincidence that Easter, which is based on earlier festivals marking the resurrection of nature at spring, is celebrated when the Sun is in this sign. The sign of Aries begins at the spring equinox and Easter is calculated as the first Sunday after the first full Moon after the spring equinox.

THREE

The Heart of the Sun

⊙ THE GLYPH FOR THE SUN IS A PERFECT CIRCLE WITH A DOT in the centre and symbolises our dual nature – earthly and eternal. The circle stands for the boundary of the personality, which distinguishes and separates each individual from every other individual, for it is our differences from other people that make us unique, not our similarities. The dot in the centre indicates the mysterious 'divine spark' within us and the potential for becoming conscious of who we truly are, where we have come from and what we may become.

The Meaning of the Sun

Each of your planets represents a different strand of your personality. The Sun is often reckoned to be the most important factor of your whole birth chart. It describes your sense of identity, and the sign that the Sun was in when you were born, your Sun sign, along with its house position and any aspects to other planets, shows how you develop and express that identity.

Your Role in Life

Each of the signs is associated with certain roles that can be played in an infinite number of ways. Take one of the roles of Aries, which is the warrior. A warrior can cover anything from Attila the Hun, who devastated vast stretches of Europe with his deliberate violence, to an eco-warrior, battling to save the environment. The role, warrior, is the same; the motivation and actions are totally different. You can live out every part of your personality in four main ways – as creator, destroyer, onlooker or victim. How you act depends on who you choose to be from the endless variations possible from the symbolism of each of your planets, but most particularly your Sun. And you do have a choice; not all Geminis are irresponsible space cadets nor is every Scorpio a sex-crazed sadist. This book aims to paint a picture of what some of your choices might be and show what choices, conscious or unconscious, some well-known people of your sign have made.

Your upbringing will have helped shape what you believe about yourself and out of those beliefs comes, automatically, behaviour to match. For example, if you believe you are a victim, you will behave like one and the world will happily oblige by victimising you. If you see yourself as a carer, life will present you with plenty to care for – and often to care about, too. If you identify yourself as an adventurer, you'll spot opportunities at every corner. If you're a winner, then you'll tend to succeed. Shift the way that you see yourself and your whole world shifts, too.

Your Vocation

Your Sun describes your major life focus. This is not always a career. As the poet Milton said: 'They also serve who only stand and wait.' It is impossible to tell from your Sun sign exactly what your calling is – there are people of all signs occupied in practically every area of life. What is important is not so much *what* you do, but the way that you do it and it is this – how you express yourself – that your Sun describes. If you spend most of your time working at an occupation or living in a situation where you can't give expression to the qualities of your Sun, or which forces you to go against the grain of your Sun's natural inclinations, then you're likely to live a life of quiet, or possibly even noisy, desperation.

On Whose Authority

Your personality, which your birth chart maps, is like a sensitive instrument that will resonate only to certain frequencies – those that are similar to its own. Your Sun shows the kind of authority that will strike a chord with you, either positively or negatively, because it is in harmony with yours. It can show how you relate to people in authority, especially your father. (It is the Moon that usually shows the relationship with your mother and home.) In adult life it can throw light onto the types of bosses you are likely to come across, and also how you could react to them. It is a major part of the maturing process to take responsibility for expressing your own authority wisely. When you do so, many of your problems with external authorities diminish or even disappear.

In a woman's chart the Sun can also describe the kind of husband she chooses. This is partly because, traditionally, a husband had legal authority over his wife. It is also because, especially in the early years of a marriage, many women choose to pour their energies into homemaking and supporting their husbands' work in the world, rather than their own, and so his career becomes her career. As an

Arien, you may find that your father, boss or husband shows either the positive or negative traits of Aries or, as is usually the case, a mixture of both – dynamic, honourable and courageous or aggressive, impatient and selfish.

Born on the Cusp

If you were born near the beginning or end of Aries, you may know that your birthday falls on the cusp, or meeting point, of two signs. The Sun, however, can only be in one sign or the other. You can find out for sure which sign your Sun is in by checking the tables on pp. 96–7.

FOUR

The Drama of Being an Aries

EACH SIGN IS ASSOCIATED WITH A CLUSTER OF ROLES THAT HAVE their own core drama or storyline. Being born is a bit like arriving in the middle of an ongoing play and slipping into a certain part. How we play our characters is powerfully shaped in early life by having to respond to the input of the other actors around us – the people that make up our families and communities. As the play of our lives unfolds, we usually become aware that there are themes which tend to repeat themselves. We may ask ourselves questions like 'Why do I always end up with all the work / caught up in fights / with partners who mistreat me / in dead-end jobs / successful but unhappy . . .?' or whatever. Interestingly, I've found that people are less likely to question the wonderful things that happen to them again and again.

The good news is that once we recognise the way we have been playing our roles, we can then use our free-will choice to do some creative rescripting, using the same character in more constructive scenarios. Even better news is that if we change, the other people in our dramas have got to make some alterations too. If you refuse to respond to the same old cues in the customary ways, they are going to have to get creative too.

A core role of Aries is the hero. A hero has a special mission, usually fraught with danger and difficulty, which only he is capable of fulfilling. He has to pit his will and his strength, and often brains, against some adversary or evil that is threatening the survival or freedom of other, more vulnerable, individuals. He can be a doctor or scientist wrestling with nature to find a cure to conquer disease, a good Samaritan braving his community's disapproval to rescue the suffering, or a solitary, defiant Chinese student stopping tanks in Tiananmen Square. He is usually a lone figure and much depends on him. The task is great and will stretch him to, and measure, the outermost limits of his powers. The greatest of heroes can also be gentle and show a deep respect, love and courtesy towards women, beauty and the frail and vulnerable. I've used the word 'he', despite the obvious fact that about half of all Ariens are women. This is because Aries energy is a strongly 'masculine' or yang energy, whether it flows through a male or a female body. Being brought up in an environment where little girls are expected to be sugar and spice and all things nice can be tough for Aries women.

It is interesting, though hardly surprising, how many Ariens are fascinated by the figure of the hero. One of the most notable is the mythologist Joseph Campbell, who wrote *The Hero with a Thousand Faces*. He and his books have inspired many filmmakers, including Steven Spielberg and George Lucas, who produced *Star Wars*, the ultimate modern heroic adventure. When Aries musician Reg Dwight changed his name to Elton John he chose as his middle name 'Hercules'.

The plot of the Aries drama always has the Arien in the

starring role opposing a powerful enemy who gives the hero a stiff run for his money, plenty of action and cliff-hanging suspense, confrontations with danger, death or defeat and in most cases a final scene where good, in the form of our hero, triumphs over evil and everybody, except the bad guy, lives happily ever after – until the next time.

Other Aries roles are the warrior, the pioneer and the daredevil. Their storylines are similar to that of the hero. There is danger afoot, an opponent or challenge to be faced (whether it is grappling with a human enemy, the power or secrets of nature or personal fears and flaws) and a prize to be won – the crown of victory, which also symbolises triumph over selfishness. Less elevated Aries types are the hell raiser, the thug, the bully and the vandal. Here Aries aggression runs riot without the healthy focus of someone or something else to serve. Your success as an Aries is bound up with the way you handle aggression, your own and other people's, and it involves identifying worthwhile challenges to get your teeth into, then throwing yourself into those, heart and soul.

How you choose to see your role will determine your behaviour. The following chapter describes some typical Aries behaviour. Remember, though, that there is no such thing as a person who is all Aries and nothing but Aries. You are much more complicated than that and other parts of your chart will modify, or may even seem to contradict, the single, but central, strand of your personality which is your Sun sign. These other sides of your nature will add colour and contrast and may restrict or reinforce your basic Aries identity. They won't, however, cancel out the challenges you face as an Aries.

FIVE

The Aries Temperament

YOU'RE A POWERHOUSE OF ENERGY, IMPACTING THE WORLD WITH a trillion volts, bubbling over with so much exuberant life it's practically impossible to restrain you. Your energy seems unlimited, making less dynamic types seem wan and weary in comparison. Rocket-fuelled out of your depths comes a powerful psychological drive: the need to prove and assert yourself through action. Once you've got an idea into your head, it's not enough just to think or talk about it. You're impelled to do something about it – NOW! With your passionate all-or-nothing attitude towards whatever you charge at, you can be totally consumed by the intensity of the present moment. You pour your heart and soul into all your undertakings. Anything less than that holds zero interest. What's worth doing is worth doing 300 per cent.

Rash and Impatient

Patience is rarely one of your virtues. With scarcely a heartbeat between thought and deed, your impulsiveness and lack of forward planning can get you into hot water on a regular basis. Actions speak louder than words in your vocabulary, and in your urgency to act you can be wilfully deaf to timely advice from more cautious mortals – and then find yourself skidding on yet another banana skin, one that everybody else had spotted miles away. With the naivety of a child and the courage of the incautious, you'll pick yourself up after your latest calamity and, uttering scarcely a whimper, throw yourself wholeheartedly into your next escapade. No use crying over spilt milk, you'll say, life's too short for regrets – let's get on with the next chapter.

Love of Challenge

Courting trouble is your lifeblood and some of your greatest pleasures in life come from doing what other people say you cannot, or must not, do. You've no fear of going out on a limb for that is where the juicy fruit is, and it's all the more enticing if it is forbidden or hard to come by. As far as you are concerned, obstacles don't exist except as challenges to be tackled gleefully. You'll boldly go where no man – or woman – has ever gone before. That's what turns you on. Throwing caution to the winds, you'll plunge straight in for the sheer excitement of the dare or the devilment. For brass neck you're hard to beat. Victoria Beckham is reported to have demanded free flights for life when her luggage went missing!

Confidence and Optimism

You seem to have complete confidence in your own abilities to master any situation, mainly because you rarely stop to think things through or weigh up the problems or consequences of what you are taking on. You respond immediately to the call to action. This can often lead you to biting off more than you can chew and promising more than you can deliver, then running yourself into exhaustion trying to cope. Your courage seems awesome because not only are you rarely cowed by fear, you actually find danger exciting, so much so that you can go out of your way to attract it. You've a fascination with pushing yourself to the limits, because you rarely know what they are until you crash into them. Hard. However, being an eternal optimist, you just dust yourself down and start all over again, audacity undented, enthusiasm intact.

Bravado and Bluff

Underneath that confident and often cocky exterior you can be quite unsure of yourself. That's why many Ariens are driven to put themselves to the test. The only means you have of getting to know yourself is from the response you get from the world outside. The way you deal with your doubts is to whistle a happy tune so that no one knows that you are – yes – afraid, not necessarily of physical dangers, but of not being potent. Then you push on with what needs to be done, regardless.

Ariens are the archetypical bad boys and girls, however old they are in years. The French have a phrase for this. They'd call you an *enfant terrible* – a dreadful child, then smile indulgently. Sometimes your behaviour is so outrageous and naively self-centred, but completely without malice, that more staid citizens can be shocked yet entranced by your escapades. You're often living out what they'd love to do – but only in their wildest dreams.

Craving for Conflict

Stressful situations bring out the best, or worst, in you. If there's no war out there, you'll set about creating one. Immature Ariens are often spoiling for a fight and can be led by the nose by anyone who taunts them or waves a provocative challenge full in their face. Litigation is a favourite sport for some Ariens. It not only guarantees a battle but also ensures that the spotlight is on them and there's an element of delicious risk and danger involved. Ambrose Bierce's definition of a lawsuit as 'a machine that you go into as a pig and come out as a sausage' is a truth that many Ariens have learned from first-hand experience. The English politician and best-selling novelist Jeffrey Archer is one such famous Aries casualty who provoked one lawsuit too many and ended up cooling his heels behind bars.

Me First

You have a clear vision of what you want and a head-down-and-charge attitude to getting it, so it's hard for you to compromise and see other people's points of view. They practically have to poke you in the eye with them for you to notice. In your rush to get ahead, you may be totally unaware that you are trampling all over other folk's plans and priorities, not to mention feelings. It is not that you are necessarily deliberately selfish, though some Ariens are undoubtedly gobsmackingly self-serving. It is more that your strongest impulse is to get directly from where you are right now to where you want to be, in the shortest possible time. All else is commentary. One of your most important lessons is to move from tunnel vision about your own projects to a wider peripheral vision which takes in the scenery around you, and that includes other people's lives.

Every sign has major lessons to learn from the sign opposite. Your opposite sign is Libra and you could do well to take a leaf out of that book when it comes to cooperation, consideration for others, reflective decision-making and strategic planning. Mix a smidgen of those in with your dynamism, energy and decisiveness, and you will not only smooth your way to success, you will also avoid the revenge of enraged former allies that is so often the downfall of the strictly me-first Aries. Remember what happened to Jason.

Temper and Temperament

Your temper is legendary and your fuse exceedingly short. It's often the petty irritations that irk you the most. William Booth, founder of the Salvation Army, who dealt daily with injustice on a colossal scale, used to make the most almighty fuss and turn the household upside down if the toast wasn't exactly to his liking. You can erupt like a volcano, sending burning lava of white-hot invective showering down on everyone within range – and it is a very wide range – with wounding words and blistering insults. Then, for you, it's over, done, finished with, full stop. It's out of your system and you can find it puzzling that other people don't treat your outburst in the same way, especially those who cast it up to you years later and make it abundantly clear that, for them, the matter is far from forgotten. This is how you can, quite unwittingly, make dangerous enemies. Smart Ariens learn to apologise in style.

The Meek Aries

Sometimes you'll come across an Arien who seems utterly charming and meek, with not a sharp elbow in sight. Take a look around and you'll spot the aggression or flamboyance somewhere in their lives, in their partners or associates or circumstances, or in their bodies as illness. The energy of your Sun sign doesn't just go away if you don't live it yourself. Somebody else will pick it up and act it out for you

and sometimes even against you. A good example is the life
of the actress Doris Day, the world's favourite virgin and as
sweet and sunny-natured as they come. It would be hard to
pick her out as an Arien, except for the fact that playing the
tomboy in *Calamity Jane* was her favourite role. But her
autobiography made clear that behind that charming,
carefree exterior was a tortured woman. Married at 17, her
first husband beat her regularly, her second was no better
and the third left her penniless, having squandered her
fortune. American jazz singer Billie Holiday was similar,
with her fatal attraction to bad boys who treated her rough.

Life's Limitations

Because you live so much in your imagination, where you
can walk through walls and speed restrictions don't apply,
coming to terms with the limitations and realities of
everyday life can be a sobering encounter for many an
Arien. This is why some sidestep that particular
confrontation at every opportunity. Learning from
experience is hard for you because the faith that it will all
work out just fine the next time round is hardwired into
your system.

Caution: Aries at Work

Ariens often find themselves on a collision course with
authority. Your relationships with your father and bosses
are often challenging ones, with swords being crossed at
regular intervals. There is something about authority that
makes you want to stand up to it. Life at work is not always
easy for young Ariens, nor indeed for their employers. It can
be hard for you to buckle down to discipline and learn to
obey somebody else's orders. Being born to lead, you know
your place. It's at the head of the procession, sabre raised,

leading the cavalry charge. You're the scout checking out new territory for potential enemies, the trailblazer clearing the way for those that follow, the knight, or Joan of Arc, in shining armour ridding the world of scoundrels and rotters. Independent to a fault, you have minimal interest in being second-in-command to anyone. With your infectious enthusiasm and ability to inspire others to give of their best, you are a first-class promoter and can indeed be the finest person around to spearhead a campaign and get any fresh enterprise off the ground.

The Dashing Sprinter

Your energy comes in quick bursts. You are built for speed but not endurance. Brilliant at starting off projects, all fired up with enthusiasm and ready to go, it's much less easy for you to finish what you've begun. You can achieve phenomenal amounts of work while your interest is held but, once the novelty has worn off, boredom can set in and quick as a flash you'll divert your attentions to something more exciting. Wise bosses will slot you into the fire-fighting jobs that are your forte. Insecure ones would much prefer to fire you.

As a boss, unless you've got a goodly helping of earth or water planets in your chart, you're not always the best judge of character, being too trusting and able to see the potential rather than the flaws in everybody. It's probably better to have other people to do the hiring. You can do the firing if need be — you're unlikely to have much of a problem with that. Administration is rarely one of your gifts either. Pick efficient underlings with asbestos suits who know that your bark is worse than your bite and who'll serve you loyally in return for the colourful drama and spontaneous generosity you bring into their lives.

Aries and Health

Aries rules the head, the adrenals and the defence system. Acting first and thinking later leaves many young Aries with some kind of head injury; and when relationships are rocky you may be prone to skin, kidney and eye problems.

Thanks to your abundant natural vitality, you're usually fighting fit and can bounce back quickly after any minor illness. Sometimes you even have too much energy and have to find an outlet for it, or you will go 'pop'. My Aries grandmother kept her house scrubbed to within an inch of its life and not only thrashed the carpets weekly, by hand, but polished under them too.

Stressful Times

Splitting headaches or full-blown migraines are often your response to unbearable stress. Stress for Ariens doesn't generally mean having too many challenges; it means being bogged down by tedium or blocked from finding a suitable outlet for your combative energy. When the going gets tough and you have to hold back on your anger, you're also prone to throwing up red, itchy rashes and unexplained inflammations in your body. Or you may get the bouts of depression, alternating with bursts of over-activity, which are typical signs of repressed Aries energy.

When ill your temperature can shoot up rapidly and develop into very high fevers. This is a healthy response. Within sensible limits it's usually best to let these run their course without suppressing them. You'll soon be fighting fit, with your immune system stronger than ever. The odd thing is that many Ariens who could enter a lion's den with barely a flicker of fear, or face serious illness with remarkable courage, can turn into complete babies and drama queens when they have to cope with a sniffle.

Keeping Healthy

You can find it boring or enraging to be trapped in a body that needs to be fed, watered and rested at regular intervals. You tend to fling food at it haphazardly and forget the most basic of maintenance. Thanks to your phenomenal recuperative powers, you can get away with that longer than most but with the bare minimum of care and attention you have a great chance of staying fit and healthy for a very long time.

Aries and the Others

There's an old joke about Aries which strongly denies the common assumption that Ariens don't notice other people. Of course they do, goes the punchline – they're the enemy. An exaggeration, of course, but there's just enough truth in it to raise a smile of recognition.

Relationships can be a difficult area for Ariens. Compromise and cooperation aren't concepts you can get your head round readily, so you're not always the easiest person to live with or work beside. You prefer to be boss and it's hard for you to accommodate other people's wishes, especially if they clash with your plans. You can often be so fired up with pushing your own agenda through instantly that what other people might want tends to get elbowed to the sidelines. That doesn't always go down too well in close relationships where the general idea is democracy not dictatorship. It usually takes a few head-on collisions until you realise, to your astonishment, that other people have their own priorities and, even more strangely, that they don't necessarily correspond to yours.

Out of Order

You can be terribly hurt if others accuse you of being pushy or insensitive, as you genuinely intend to act in everybody's best interests. The problem is that others usually prefer to be consulted about what those interests might be. Some unpolished Ariens ride roughshod over weaker characters and then despise them for not sticking up for themselves. You're usually at your best with an equal partner who isn't afraid to pull you up sharply when you step over the line, because frequently you haven't a clue where that line lies. It is reported that when Lord Archer, an Arien given to frequent breaches of social niceties, began to act out of order his wife Mary would simply look at him pointedly and say 'Jeffrey!' and, meek as a lamb, he behaved himself. Underneath all of your brashness, you aren't as confident as you seem and can secretly fret that people might not like you. A loving partner can give you what you most need and desire, straight and honest feedback about how you are doing and loyal support when the going gets rocky.

Bores at Chores

Being wired up for war and not for washing up, you can get quite irked at having to tackle the boring necessities of everyday life. The expectation that you should do the ironing or balance the budget can seem like a personal affront. In your heart of hearts you believe that heroes don't hoover. This is why so many Ariens gravitate towards practical partners to smooth their way and mop up after them. Consequently, if your mate isn't careful you can wriggle your way out of doing your fair share at home and so start a cold war on the domestic front. A wise partner will appeal to your inborn sense of chivalry or present the task as a challenge. A quiet word in your ear that a competitor does it better or quicker can have you on the offensive, wielding polish and duster like a sword and shield. Those adverts on television selling cleaning products declaring war on germs and dirt have a suspiciously Arien ring to them.

True Romance

You tend to dramatise everything about your life and your relationships are no exceptions. You are apt to develop passionate crushes and then worship from afar. It's often a case of the more unattainable the object of your affections, the more desirable they become. You love the thrill of the chase and the brief triumph of capture, but unless there is something substantial to hold your attention you can quickly tire of your trophy. Then, without so much as a backward glance, you'll go galloping off in pursuit of yet another fair maiden or knight. But if the tables are turned and someone chases you, it's more than likely you'll bolt. You prefer to be the hunter, not the hunted. When you are genuinely in love, though, it's a different story. You don't just fall in love, you're in there truly, madly, deeply. Aries is a magically romantic sign. When you've met the right partner, you'll go to almost any lengths to woo and to win him or her. You're capable of deep and lasting loyalty and make a wonderfully tender and attentive lover.

Aries and Sex

Hot-blooded and passionate, Ariens love sex. It doesn't take much to turn you on and when you want someone, you want them urgently. You can't get fired up until your imagination is fully stimulated, though. Fortunately for you, and your partner, your brain is a highly active and creative sex organ that rarely switches off, so your libido is usually pulsating with power. It probably won't surprise you to learn that Casanova had his Sun in Aries.

Ariens can be blatant exponents of the double standard.

If your eyes stray elsewhere, it's brushed off as a little harmless fun. Woe betide your partner if they allow themselves the same freedom. That is classed as high treason.

There's a youthful quality about most Ariens that can be enchanting and exciting, and there can be a tendency to carry on with adolescent behaviour through mid-life and beyond. Some Ariens end up as the oldest swingers in town. Age might play havoc with the equipment but it certainly does nothing to wither your sex drive. Arien lothario Hugh Hefner sees no reason to give up his limo-loads of glamorous escorts just because he is getting on a bit, and indeed, why should he? Hefner is perfectly upfront in praising the virtues of Viagra. Where there's an Aries will (or willy!) around, there's sure to be a way.

SIX

Aspects of the Sun

PLANETS, JUST LIKE PEOPLE, CAN HAVE IMPORTANT RELATIONSHIPS with each other. These relationships are called aspects. Aspects to your Sun from any other planet can influence your personality markedly. The most powerful effects come with those from the slower-moving planets – Saturn, Uranus, Neptune or Pluto. Sometimes they can alter your ideas about yourself and your behaviour patterns so much that you may not feel at all typical of your sign in certain areas of your life.

Check if your birth date and year appear in the various sections below to find out if one or more of these planets was aspecting the Sun when you were born. Only the so-called challenging aspects have been included. These are formed when the planets are together, opposite or at right angles to each other in the sky.

Unfortunately, because space is restricted, other aspects have been left out, although they have similar effects to those described below and, for the same reason, a few dates will inevitably have been missed out, too. (You can find out for sure whether or not your Sun is aspected at my website www.janeridderpatrick.com) If your Sun has no aspects to

39

Saturn, Uranus, Neptune or Pluto, you're more likely to be a typical Arien.

Some well-known Ariens with challenging aspects to their Suns appear below. You can find more in the birthday section at the end of the book.

Sun in Aries in Aspect with Saturn
If you were born between 1937 and 1939, 1967 and 1969 or 1996 and 1998, whether or not your birthday is listed below, you are likely to feel the influence of Saturn on your Sun.

20–30 March in: 1937–8, 1945, 1951–2, 1959, 1967, 1974, 1981, 1988, and 1996
31 March–10 April in: 1938–9, 1946, 1952, 1960, 1968, 1975, 1982, 1989 and 1997
11–20 April in: 1931–2, 1938–40, 1946–7, 1953, 1961, 1969, 1976, 1982–3, 1990 and 1998

Jeffrey Archer	Roger Bannister	Doris Day
Clare Francis	David Frost	Ruby Wax

Your slow-burning ambition is to prove yourself and make your mark on the world. The underlying doubt that Ariens normally experience about being inadequate can be magnified in you into a nagging and undermining fear of failure. Often Ariens with this aspect have been either overlooked in childhood or made to feel by their fathers or teachers that their efforts were insignificant. Their fathers may also have been stern and successful or disappointed or disappointing men.

To prove, to yourself as much as anybody else, that you don't care, you may challenge or even attack people in authority and refuse to submit to discipline. You are quite capable of acting so provocatively that they are practically forced to retaliate by disapproval and dismissal. This then reinforces your belief that all authority stinks and makes you even more difficult the next time round. And so it goes on, until you see your own part in the proceedings, and hopefully mend your ways.

Alternatively you may be an ambitious high achiever, driven by the need to win and to climb up the ladder of whatever establishment you aspire to. Your real challenge, however, is not to fight authorities or race to get their approval. It is to wrestle with that judge inside your head that drips out discouraging messages about your not being good enough. This takes courage, but when you face squarely your own inner bogey of self-doubt you can build up a solid sense of who you are and what you want to be – then, regardless of what anybody else might think, go about disciplining yourself to do whatever it takes to get there. This is your guaranteed road to success, achievement and social recognition.

Sun in Aries in Aspect with Uranus

If you were born between 1927 and 1935, whether or not your birthday is listed below, you are likely to feel the influence of Uranus on your Sun.

20–30 March in: 1928–30, 1950–3, 1969–71 and 1987–91
31 March–10 April in: 1930–3, 1951–5, 1971–3 and 1990–4
11–20 April in: 1933–6, 1954–7, 1972–5 and 1992–6

Victoria Beckham	Erich von Daniken	Bette Davis
Rolf Harris	Ewan McGregor	Steve McQueen

The only mould you are willing to fit into is one of your own making. This can be a potentially explosive mixture, producing the rebel with or without a cause. Your highest priority could be to improve whatever system you are up against by challenging and overthrowing, or reforming, whatever is unjust or hidebound in the accepted way of doing things. You have an enormous contribution to make to changing life for everyone, including yourself, for the better but there are one or two cautions. Both Uranus and the Sun in Aries can be impulsive and overlook the opinions and feelings of other people. You may have strong fixed ideas of how things should be and push forward relentlessly to activate them. There can be a tendency to assume that just because you *know* that an idea or plan is the one true one that it is so, and that everyone else must and should agree with you. You can be hugely self-willed and can be difficult and, on occasion, downright bloody-minded. But without this conviction you would not have the drive to carry your ideas through. It may feel as if you are swimming against the tide at times with some of your notions, but it is often nearer to the mark to say that your ways of thinking and acting may be well ahead of their time – and occasionally more than a little potty. Erich von Daniken's books, like *Chariots of the Gods*, about alien landings on Earth have attracted both enthusiastic followers and the derision of sceptics. More than most Ariens, you need a career and relationship which present variety and challenges or you could end up sabotaging one or both through sheer boredom.

Sun in Aries in Aspect with Neptune

20–30 March in: 1942–9 and 1983–9
31 March–10 April in: 1946–52 and 1987–94
11–20 April in: 1950–6 and 1992–9

William Booth	Robbie Coltrane	Diana Ross
Aretha Franklin	Emmylou Harris	Elton John

The combination of the upfront warrior energies of an Aries Sun and those of soft-focused and self-sacrificing

Neptune is not always an easy one to live with. Some Ariens with this combination come across more like wistful lambs than battling rams – a bit like Robbie Coltrane's character, Hagrid, in the Harry Potter films. It can be tempting to put most of your energies into dodging problems and avoiding confrontation. It's hard to pin you down, either physically or emotionally. You may prefer to live in your fantasies or inner life rather than facing the outside world, which you often find coarse and harsh in contrast to your sense of how life should be. There may be a strongly spiritual or devotional side to your nature. Others may see only the image they have of you, rather than the real you. Often you're not sure who you are yourself.

Ariens need to fight for something, but with this aspect you can feel guilty, helpless and confused if you push yourself forward. You can feel you have neither the right, nor the might, to do so. It's important to find some area in your life where you feel that you are championing an important and worthwhile cause, preferably sticking up for the underdog, the outcast or the vulnerable. Then the very finest qualities of this aspect can blossom and there will be no holds barred in fighting the good fight with all your might. William Booth, founder of the aptly named Salvation Army, is a perfect example of this. You also need to learn to say no – firmly – as you tend to take on far too much because you can easily feel guilty and over-responsible. Do be careful, though, when the going gets rough, not to lose yourself in alcohol or food as you may be prone to allergies and addictions.

Sun in Aries in Aspect with Pluto

20–30 March in: 1920–5 and 1971–7
31 March–10 April in: 1923–31 and 1975–81
11–20 April in: 1924, 1931–9 and 1979–84

| Maya Angelou | Jeffrey Archer | Joan Bakewell |
| Marlon Brando | Rev. Ian Paisley | Dusty Springfield |

You are certainly a force to be reckoned with. No one can accuse you of lack of determination. Your will is formidable. When you set your mind on some course of action, nobody and nothing is going to be allowed to stand in your way. Sometimes you believe that attack is the best form of defence. Be careful, though, not to come on too strong; some people could mistake it for bullying. You can go to extremes to get your own way. (To prevent the cameras straying to his obese bottom half, Marlon Brando refuses to be filmed unless naked from the waist down.)

Careers which demand stamina, endurance and a strong sense of purpose suit you well: work involving money, power, sex, secrets or birth and death has a special appeal. James D. Watson shared a Nobel Prize for his groundbreaking discovery of the structure of DNA, the molecule that controls living matter. You have an urge to push back the boundaries harder and stronger than most other Ariens. The challenge of this aspect is to learn to use your will honourably and wisely. When things get tough you just pull out the plug on your old life and re-invent yourself. Misuse of power can enrage you and your courage in confronting this can be awe-inspiring. You can be secretive and defensive, feeling that you need to protect yourself from being invaded or overpowered, though from exactly what you may not be sure. Sadly for some, their mistrust, because of past experience, has a basis in fact. When she was eight Maya Angelou, at the hands of her mother's boyfriend, suffered terrible abuse, which made her withdraw into herself for years. You can play your cards close to your chest about your ambitions for fear of loss or attack if you give too much away about yourself. It's important that you check your suspicions against reality. Life's a lot safer than you think.

SEVEN

Meeting Your Moon

D THE GLYPH FOR THE MOON IS THE SEMI-CIRCLE OR CRESCENT. It is a symbol for the receptiveness of the soul and is associated with feminine energies and the ebb and flow of the rhythms of life. In some Islamic traditions it represents the gateway to paradise and the realms of bliss.

The Sun and Moon are the two complementary poles of your personality, like yang and yin, masculine and feminine, active and reflective, career and home, father and mother. The Moon comes into its own as a guide at night, the time of sleeping consciousness. It also has a powerful effect on the waters of the earth. Likewise, the Moon in your birth chart describes what you respond to instinctively and feel 'in your waters', often just below the level of consciousness. It is your private radar system, sending you messages via your body responses and feelings, telling you whether a situation seems safe or scary, nice or nasty. Feelings provide vital information about circumstances in and around you. Ignore them at your peril; that will lead you into emotional, and sometimes even physical, danger. Eating disorders tend to be associated with being out of touch with, or neglecting, the instincts and the body, both of which the Moon describes.

Extraordinary though it might seem to those who are emotionally tuned in, some people have great difficulty in knowing what they are feeling. One simple way is to pay attention to your body. Notice any sensations that attract your attention. Those are linked to your feelings. Now get a sense of whether they are pleasant or unpleasant, then try to put a more exact name to what those feelings might be. Is it sadness, happiness, fear? What is it that they are trying to tell you? Your Moon hints at what will strongly activate your feelings. Learning to trust and decode this information will help make the world seem – and be – a safer place.

The Moon represents your drive to nurture and protect yourself and others. Its sign, house and aspects describe how you respond and adapt emotionally to situations and what feeds you, in every sense of the word. It gives information about your home and home life and how you experienced your mother, family and childhood, as well as describing your comfort zone of what feels familiar – the words 'family' and 'familiar' come from the same source. It shows, too, what makes you feel secure and what could comfort you when you're feeling anxious. Your Moon describes what moves and motivates you powerfully at the deepest instinctual level and indicates what is truly the 'matter' in – or with – your life.

Knowing children's Moon signs can help parents and teachers better understand their insecurities and respect their emotional make-up and needs, and so prevent unnecessary hurt, or even harm, to sensitive young lives. It's all too easy to expect that our children and parents should have the same emotional wiring as we do, but that's rarely how life works. Finding our parents' Moon signs can be a real revelation. It can often help us understand where they are coming from, what they need and why they react to us in the way they do. Many of my clients have been able to find the understanding and compassion to forgive their parents when they realised that they were doing their very best with the emotional resources available to them.

In relationships it is important that your Moon's requirements are met to a good enough extent. For example, if you have your Moon in Sagittarius you must have adventure, freedom and the opportunity to express your beliefs. If being with your partner constantly violates these basic needs, you will never feel secure and loved and the relationship could, in the long term, undermine you. However, if your Moon feels too comfortable, you will never change and grow. The art is to get a good working balance between support and challenge.

A man's Moon sign can show some of the qualities he will unconsciously select in a wife or partner. Some of the others are shown in his Venus sign. Many women can seem much more like their Moon signs than their Sun signs, especially if they are involved in mothering a family and being a support system for their husbands or partners. It is only at the mid-life crisis that many women start to identify more with the qualities of their own Suns rather than living that out through their partners' ambitions. Similarly, men tend to live out the characteristics of their Moon signs through their wives and partners until mid-life, often quite cut off from their own feelings and emotional responses. If a man doesn't seem at all like his Moon sign, then check out the women in his life. There's a good chance that his wife, mother or daughter will show these qualities.

Your Moon can be in any sign, including the same one as your Sun. Each sign belongs to one of the four elements: Fire, Earth, Air or Water. The element of your Moon can give you a general idea of how you respond to new situations and what you need to feel safe and comforted. We all become anxious if our Moon's needs are not being recognised and attended to. We then, automatically, go into our personal little rituals for making ourselves feel better. Whenever you are feeling distressed, especially when you are way out of your comfort zone in an unfamiliar situation, do something to feed and soothe your Moon. You're almost certain to calm down quickly.

Fire Moons

If you have a fire Moon in Aries, Leo or Sagittarius, your first response to any situation is to investigate in your imagination the possibilities for drama, excitement and self-expression. Feeling trapped by dreary routine in an ordinary humdrum life crushes you completely. Knowing that you are carrying out a special mission feeds your soul. To you, all the world's a stage and a voyage of discovery. Unless you are at the centre of the action playing some meaningful role, anxiety and depression can set in. To feel secure, you have to have an appropriate outlet for expressing your spontaneity, honourable instincts and passionate need to be of unique significance. The acknowledgement, appreciation and feedback of people around you are essential, or you don't feel real. Not to be seen and appreciated, or to be overlooked, can feel like a threat to your very existence.

Earth Moons

If you have an earth Moon in Taurus, Virgo or Capricorn, you'll respond to new situations cautiously and practically. Rapidly changing circumstances where you feel swept along and out of control are hard for you to cope with. You need time for impressions to sink in. Sometimes it is only much later, after an event has taken place, that you become sure what you felt about it. Your security lies in slowing down, following familiar routines and rituals, even if they are a bit obsessive, and focusing on something, preferably material – possibly the body itself or nature – which is comforting because it is still there. Indulging the senses in some way often helps too, through food, sex or body care. So does taking charge of the practicalities of the immediate situation, even if this is only mixing the drinks or passing out clipboards. To feel secure, you need continuity and a sense that you have your hand on the rudder of your own life. Think of the rather irreverent joke about the man seeming to cross himself in a crisis, all the while actually touching his most valued possessions to check that they are still intact – spectacles, testicles, wallet and watch. That must have been thought up by someone with the Moon in an earth sign.

Air Moons

When your Moon is in an air sign – Gemini, Libra or Aquarius – you feel most secure when you can stand back from situations and observe them from a distance. Too much intimacy chokes you and you'll tend to escape it by going into your head to the safety of ideas and analysis. Even in close relationships you need your mental, and preferably physical, space. You often have to think, talk or write about what you are feeling before you are sure what your feelings are. By putting them 'out there' so that you can examine them clearly, you can claim them as your own. Unfairness and unethical behaviour can upset you badly and make you feel uneasy until you have done something about it or responded in some way. It can be easy with an air Moon to be unaware of, or to ignore, your own feelings because you are more responsive to ideas, people and situations outside of yourself that may seem to have little connection with you. This is not a good idea, as it cuts you off from the needs of your body as well as your own emotional intelligence. Making opportunities to talk, play with and exchange ideas and information can reduce the stress levels if anxiety strikes.

Water Moons

Finally, if your Moon is in a water sign – Cancer, Scorpio or Pisces – you are ultra-sensitive to atmospheres, and you can experience other people's pain or distress as if they were your own. You tend to take everything personally and, even if the situation has nothing at all to do with you, feel responsible for making it better. Your worst nightmare is to feel no emotional response coming back from other people. That activates your deep-seated terror of abandonment, which can make you feel that you don't exist and is, quite literally, what you fear even more than death. If you feel insecure, you may be tempted to resort to emotional manipulation to try to force intimacy with others – not a good idea, as this can lead to the very rejection that you dread. You are at your most secure when the emotional climate is positive and you have trusted, supportive folk around who will winkle you out of hiding if you become too reclusive. With a water Moon, it is vital to learn to value your own feelings and to take them seriously – and to have a safe, private place you can retreat to when you feel emotionally fragile. As you never forget anything which has made a feeling impression on you, sometimes your reactions are triggered by unconscious memories of things long past, rather than what is taking place in the present. When you learn to interpret them correctly, your feelings are your finest ally and will serve you well.

Finding Your Moon Sign

If you don't yet know your Moon sign, before looking it up, you could have some fun reading through the descriptions that follow and seeing if you can guess which one it is. To find your Moon sign, check your year and date of birth in the tables on p. 98–111. For a greater in-depth understanding of your Moon sign, you might like to read about its characteristics in the book in this series about that sign.

At the beginning of each section are the names of some well-known Ariens with that particular Moon sign. You can find more about them in Chapter Ten.

Sun in Aries with Moon in Aries

Robert Carlyle	Marlon Brando	Rodney King
Ali MacGraw	Annie Sullivan	Kenneth Tynan

With your Sun and Moon in the same sign, you are what is known as a double Aries, and that can often be translated as double trouble. Hot-tempered, impulsive and bossy, you tend to live for the moment, throwing yourself passionately into the action at hand. You thrive on challenge, the tougher the better as far as you are concerned. It's best if you can find some worthwhile causes to champion – like Annie Sullivan, who succeeded in teaching blind and deaf Helen Keller to university standard – otherwise all that fighting energy can get used up in senseless squabbles and scrapes, or converted into physical symptoms like headaches. Boredom and a peaceful humdrum life would be intolerable to you. You can be sure that action will come your way, fortunately rarely as violently as in the case of black motorist, Rodney King. He was brutally beaten by

Los Angeles police officers who were acquitted despite the incident being filmed. Mass rioting followed this miscarriage of justice, leaving 58 people dead and 2000 injured. You are a rebel to the core and it would be surprising if you haven't had some stormy run-ins with those in authority. Theatre critic Kenneth Tynan caused an uproar when he became the first person to use the 'f' word on the BBC. You need to be careful not to be high-handed, as it's not always easy for you to appreciate other people's points of view. You are not exactly subtle and can be a tad insensitive when it comes to other people's agendas or feelings but you're the best possible person to have around where there are barricades in need of storming. As insecurity can make you belligerent, strenuous physical exercise could be just the thing to restore some calm when the going gets tough.

Sun in Aries with Moon in Taurus

| Karen Blixen | Robert Downey Jr | Elton John |
| James Lovell | Gregory Peck | Diana Ross |

Your need for stability can often mean that you cultivate caution and common sense more than most Ariens. Peace matters to you, and you are willing to fight for it and enforce it if need be. With your energy, drive and enterprise, coupled with staying power and sound business instincts, you have what it takes to ground your vision and produce concrete and lasting results. You can be a tower of strength in a tight corner. When a serious explosion left Apollo 13 stranded in space without electricity, light or water, astronaut James Lovell coolly reported 'Houston, we've got a problem', then managed successfully to guide the Command Module on its hazardous trip back to Earth.

Security for you lies in the simple things in life – owning your own home, a full bank account and stomach, satisfaction in bed and, above all, a sense of being in control. Events moving too fast can leave you feeling anxious and you may divert a great deal of energy into keeping things the same that might better be allowed to change. It's important to check whether your perspective is correct or whether fear is making you stubborn. When insecure, the urge to accumulate or domineer can become a bit obsessive. You may then shop with a vengeance or feed your sensual appetites in an attempt to feel better. Real security, however, lies in developing a solid sense of your own worth which cannot be bought or borrowed. It also means learning to step off the roundabout at regular intervals and recharging your batteries at the slow pace of your own heartbeat. If you feel stressed out, an hour or two in the garden tackling tree roots and termites would do you the world of good.

Sun in Aries with Moon in Gemini

Marilyn Ferguson	Bette Davis	Doris Day
Ewan McGregor	Spike Milligan	Omar Sharif

You could talk the hind legs off a donkey and as a child probably drove your parents crazy with constant questions about why, where, what and when – and how can words take the legs from donkeys? Looking for thrills at every turn, you're the nearest thing to a human perpetual motion machine, with mouth and muscles rarely still. Running on so much nervous energy, it's hard for you to know when enough is enough and to take a break. Your incredible dynamism and energy can get scattered, as it is easy for you to lose focus and fritter away your stamina. Incurably curious, and sometimes downright nosy, with your low boredom threshold, you need a career that offers high-tension drama and plenty of change.

You're a live wire and charmer with a taste for danger and you can twist just about anybody round your little finger. Anarchic comedian Spike Milligan, who pioneered the joke without the punchline, irritated by the smarm coming his way at an awards ceremony, brought the house down with his aside – 'grovelling little bastard' – about Prince Charles' accolade. (He apologised later and was forgiven, as the two were good friends.) You'd much prefer to be the free spirit who never grows up. With a Gemini Moon, you may prefer two places to call your homes. You'll love the fun of playing with children but the responsibilities and constant grind of domesticity could feel like a ball and chain, crippling your style and your soul. Being able to communicate is as essential to you as breathing and keeping a journal or having close friends to share your troubles and triumphs with can be useful tools in your emotional first-aid kit.

Sun in Aries with Moon in Cancer

Jeffrey Archer	Ian Duncan Smith	Aretha Franklin
William Hague	Emma Thompson	Ruby Wax

There's a tension between the urge to go out and conquer the world and a timid fearfulness that can make you want to climb back into bed and pull the covers over your head. Those whose emotional needs were fostered as a child, and were given a sense of belonging and acceptance, will find the confidence more easily to take on all comers; Jeffrey Archer certainly had a very supportive mother. Without the safety net of emotional, financial and domestic security to fall back on, you can become quite ungrounded. You can be – and need – a loyal and dedicated partner; your finest qualities come together when you tune into the needs and fears of those more vulnerable than you and fight to protect and care for them.

You are highly intuitive and, having the common touch, can quickly pick up on the feelings of those around, which gives you an excellent rapport with others. Despite the fact that they know they'll be sent up, comedian Ruby Wax manages to create a wickedly conspiratorial intimacy with her 'victims'.

Being overly touchy, it is all too easy for you to take criticism, real or imagined, far too personally and either fly into a tantrum or withdraw into sulky blame and resentment. This Aries and Cancer mix can, under stress, become childishly self-absorbed and tyrannical. If you notice yourself heading in this direction it is often best to go off somewhere alone, lick your wounds, mope despondently and exaggerate your outraged feelings until you've worked it out of your system and can finally laugh at your own dramatics. You'll then be ready to come back and join the world, refreshed and ready to tackle any dragon that crosses your path.

Sun in Aries with Moon in Leo

| Chris Evans | Olivia Hussey | Andrew Lloyd Webber |
| Graham Norton | Peter Ustinov | Vivienne Westwood |

Attention and controversy turn you on. You are a natural leader, more often than not of the opposition. With your larger-than-life personality, you are the belle of the ball and the star of the show; there is no way you won't be noticed. Could anyone possibly overlook the cheeky and outrageously camp TV host Graham Norton? Ambition and self-promotion usually come easily to you. Confidence and pizzazz ooze out of every pore and it would rarely occur to you that you might be wrong. In the quiet of your own heart you sometimes have moments of self-doubt but they tend to be fleeting. You need a place where you can shine. Any career that promises glamour, prestige and competition or, better still, a darned good fight as well, is just the job for you. Daring and confident, who can resist you? You want your own way, and you want to be loved. With the tenacity and loyalty of your Leo Moon, you are much more suited to long-haul action, and to fidelity, than many other Ariens. As you need to feel special and hate seeing yourself presented in a bad light, you usually prefer to act honourably.

You can be generous to a fault, if a bit imperious. A tendency to be patronising or take yourself rather too seriously may have to be checked. Unfortunately it is all too easy for you not to notice other people's sensitivities and agendas and if everything isn't going your way temper tantrums can quickly erupt. When you're feeling insecure you may start to show off, but by daring to be yourself you are a heart-warming inspiration to others, encouraging them to be true to themselves too.

Sun in Aries with Moon in Virgo

St Teresa of Avila	Robbie Coltrane	Emmylou Harris
Harry Houdini	J.P. Morgan	William Morris

You are likely to be rather less impulsive than other Ariens, preferring to have a good long look before making the leap. How things work can fascinate you and men with this combination are often found lovingly laying out the guts of their cars or machinery in neat little rows. You like to do things with precision and orderly rituals, even simple ones like making sure your banknotes are all the same way round, or squeezing exactly the right amount of toothpaste onto your toothbrush, can be immensely comforting in times of stress. You've a sharp eye for flaws and problem-solving is your particular gift. Harry Houdini made a career out of finding ways of escaping from any kind of restraint – even padlocked underwater boxes. Some with this combination are highly-strung and irritable and can be fault-finding fuss-pots or carping critics when under stress.

Work that is of service or leads to some clearly defined end result helps keep you grounded. The socialist craftsman William Morris advised, 'Have nothing in your houses that you do not know to be useful or believe to be beautiful.' A well-crafted task creates a sense of satisfaction and you'll go to endless trouble to sort out the details and get a job right. Theories rarely interest you unless they lead to useful results. Practical action is what appeals. Sometimes the craftsman-like quality of the Virgo Moon comes out as craftiness. Banker J.P. Morgan once said, 'I don't want a lawyer to tell me what I can't do; I hire him to tell me how to do what I want to do.' Virgo is the sign of purification and the simple life. You're unlikely, though, to go as far as St Teresa, who advocated extremes of poverty, austerity and solitude.

Sun in Aries with Moon in Libra

Maya Angelou	Richard Chamberlain	Bobby Moore
Simone Signoret	Gloria Swanson	Paul Theroux

An Arien who finds it hard to make a decision seems like a contradiction in terms, but you live with that contradiction daily. Your need to be fair and to be liked can pull you back from resolute action and you can find yourself blowing hot and cold and see-sawing between charm and aggression and altruism and feeling hard-done-by. However, even when you are attacking someone you usually manage to do it with maximum charm and minimum offence. You can have the best of both worlds if you first reflect on what is the fair and honourable solution for all involved, not forgetting to include yourself in the final equation. Then put your heart and mind into acting on that judgment.

With your love of grace and beauty, you're rather like the Samurai warriors who equipped themselves for war and peace, carrying with them their flower-arranging kits as well as their weapons. Relationships are of the utmost importance to you and it is hard for you to be without a partner – romantic or sparring. Coming up against the darker side of human nature can be a nasty shock for you, though, as you are deeply romantic and idealistic.

You've the ability to see everybody's viewpoint, yet you've an equally strong will to have your own way. Your keen sense of justice and unfairness will rouse you to put your considerable energy into righting the balance. Like Maya Angelou, you believe 'We should always be at war with injustice. Always.' Too nice is as bad as too nasty; if things become too cosy and agreeable you'll stir up controversy, then have the pleasure of smoothing down any ruffled feathers.

Sun in Aries with Moon in Scorpio

Warren Beatty	Charlie Chaplin	Julie Christie
Clare Francis	David Frost	Eddie Murphy

No one can beat you for sheer grit and determination once you have made up your mind to do something. Your Aries Sun loves a challenge and your Scorpio Moon fuels you up to hold on in there until you've completed it. Clare Francis had what it took to compete in some of the world's most demanding boat races and to sail single-handedly across the Atlantic, not a feat for sissies. You make a rock-solid friend but a formidable foe, as you can be fearless about tackling anything you feel stinks of hypocrisy or corruption. You may need to learn to keep your temper under control, especially as you are prone to jealousy and could veer towards paranoia from time to time. It's best to run your suspicions through a reality check before lashing out.

Sex and power can drive you, sometimes obsessively. Charlie Chaplin was known for his taste for young girls and, before he settled down, Warren Beatty was famous for his little black book. When he wanted a date, he would systematically work his way through it until he found someone free to be with him – and was sometimes still dialling at 2 a.m. Behind his playboy image, though, is a man serious and even passionate about political power.

You probably radiate charisma and smouldering sexuality and could find that people are drawn magnetically towards you. You tend to be quite secretive about your true feelings, revealing them only when you are absolutely sure you can trust your confidant, or never at all. Warren Beatty, to his credit, has always remained clam-like about his love life. He wasn't the one who kissed and told.

Sun in Aries with Moon in Sagittarius

Dirk Bogarde	Giacomo Casanova	Viktor Frankl
Vincent van Gogh	Kitty Kelley	Erich Fromm

Outspoken Aries with sassy Sagittarius means that nobody is going to be left in the dark about your opinions. You say it like it is with utter sincerity and foot-in-the-mouth naivety, then wonder why people get upset. Many with this combination are drawn to teaching and preaching. Van Gogh was once a travelling evangelist, sleeping on floors and giving away his possessions. You want to understand the meaning of life, then spread your philosophy widely. Psychologist Victor Frankl found the will to survive the horrors of the Nazi death camps by imagining himself lecturing to students about lessons gained from his experiences. This he eventually did, teaching that it is the meaning we give to events, not the events themselves, that determine our lives.

You may be a wild child with itchy feet and wanderlust. A born rover, in love with the adventure of life, you're constantly in search of a widening horizon. Many of you with this Moon may prefer, like Dirk Bogarde, to live abroad, for part of your life at least. Fidelity may not come easily to you because of your hunger for conquest and the unknown. Sexual adventurer Casanova frolicked through the bedrooms of European high society and later wrote his scandalous and highly embroidered memoirs from prison. You need a partner who can share your enthusiasms and will give you plenty of freedom. Housekeeping is rarely your forte; your fridge could overflow with wilted leftovers, bought in an extravagant party-mood moment. Generous to a fault, you probably love splashing cash around. Your worst nightmare is being tied down and bored, and not allowed out to play.

Aries Sun with Moon in Capricorn

Otto von Bismarck	Joan Bakewell	John Major
Sarah Jessica Parker	Elliot Ness	Paloma Picasso

Highly ambitious, you will put your considerable energy into achieving your goals and ensuring you acquire the status, power and respect you crave. Hard work is as familiar to you as breathing. Many with this combination, like John Major, have come from poor or humble backgrounds and work their way steadily to the top or, like Bismarck, were raised in homes where correct behaviour and discipline were the rule, rather than spontaneity and warm acceptance. There's a bonus in this: you are well able to look after yourself and, unless you give in to the periodic depression that can dog you, you're headed straight up the ladder of success.

The nagging fear that you'll be rejected unless you behave in a certain way to please those you see as your superiors can keep you chronically insecure until you become part of the establishment yourself. Ariens generally perform poorly as politicians because of their recklessness, lack of staying power and need to challenge the system. Those with Capricorn Moons tend to be the exception. You fight to become part of the system. This is a useful combination for creating success in the media and business, as you're an idealist yet a realist. You make a loyal and responsible partner if you can resist the temptation to put your home life in second place to your ambitions. Oddly, solitude and sinking into melancholy feed you, so it is important to allow yourself to indulge in them from time to time, as well as taking time off to enjoy the fruits of your considerable labours too.

Sun in Aries with Moon in Aquarius

| Joan Crawford | Russell Crowe | Penelope Keith |
| Steve McQueen | Debbie Reynolds | Tennessee Williams |

It is not always easy for you to know what you are feeling and your moods can be quite contrary. One moment you may be abrupt and withdrawn, and the next you'll be chatty and friendly. Others may see you as aloof and possibly even a bit of an oddball or loner. You can be a brilliant strategist and, being much more of a team player than most other Ariens, you enjoy being part of a group with some common purpose. Many with this combination have a strong social conscience and put their mouths, money and muscle at the service of their chosen cause. Steve McQueen used to cream off perks, like clothes, from filmsets and donate them to a reform school where he himself had spent a few years.

You like things logical and clear-cut. Messy emotions disturb you, your own just as much as other people's. You're more at ease with loyal friendships than intimacy and if anybody tries to get too close, either physically or emotionally, you'll start to feel jittery and trapped. Your domestic arrangements may be unusual or unconventional in some way, with people coming and going. Even if you have lived in the same house all your life, you may feel as though you're in a transit camp, slightly on edge waiting for the call to move on. (At a low-point in her career Debbie Reynolds did camp quite literally – in a Cadillac.) This underlying sense of impermanence can stop you rooting emotionally anywhere, putting pressure on relationships. Deep down you feel the whole world is your family and for contentment you need to find some way of opening and widening your family home or circle to let in the world. Time on your own as well as with friends is essential to recharge your batteries.

Sun in Aries with Moon in Pisces

| Betty Ford | Hugh Hefner | Mistinguett |
| Chico Marx | Piers Morgan | Dusty Springfield |

One part of you enjoys confrontation while another will evade it at all costs, fudging facts if need be. Chico Marx claimed, when his wife caught him kissing another woman, that he wasn't kissing her, he was only whispering in her mouth. Escaping from everyday reality at frequent intervals is essential for your well-being and you may be rather reclusive. Your are a dreamer, longing to lose yourself in seamless bliss. Playboy boss Hugh Hefner has the financial wherewithal to create his own version of paradise on earth in his fantasy mansion shielded from the realities, limitations and rejections of the real world. He ships in glamorous playmates in bulk and replaces them at regular intervals when the glitter wears off. For some Ariens, the sensitivity and dependency of this Moon can be unbearable and they erect a barrier of cynicism to shut out their own easily bruised feelings.

Your best qualities come when you fight for those whom mainstream life has cast off. Betty Ford, wife of US President Gerald Ford, did just that. With immense courage, given her exposed public position, she spoke openly about her own drug, drink and health problems and went on to found a centre for drug dependents. With a heart that bleeds for the unfortunate, you empathise instinctively with other people's pain. You feel guilty and uncomfortable until you have supplied what it is you sense they need. As a child, you probably learned to read emotional atmospheres in order to have your own needs met indirectly. Media figures with Pisces Moons, like tabloid editor Piers Morgan, can tune into, and cater for, the controversy and sensationalism that large numbers of people are hungry for and so capture the public imagination to great advantage.

EIGHT

Mercury – It's All in the Mind

THE GLYPHS FOR THE PLANETS ARE MADE UP OF THREE SYMBOLS: the circle, the semi-circle and the cross. Mercury is the only planet, apart from Pluto, whose glyph is made up of all three of these symbols. At the bottom there is the cross, representing the material world; at the top is the semi-circle of the crescent Moon, symbolising the personal soul; and in the middle, linking these two, is the circle of eternity, expressed through the individual. In mythology, Mercury was the only god who had access to all three worlds – the underworld, the middle world of earth and the higher world of the gods. Mercury in your chart represents your ability, through your thoughts and words, to make connections between the inner world of your mind and emotions, the outer world of other people and events, and the higher world of intuition. Your Mercury sign can give you a great deal of information about the way your mind works and about your interests, communication skills and your preferred learning style.

It can be frustrating when we just can't get through to some people and it's easy to dismiss them as being either completely thick or deliberately obstructive. Chances are they are neither. It may be that you're simply not talking each other's languages. Knowing your own and other people's communication styles can lead to major breakthroughs in relationships.

Information about children's natural learning patterns can help us teach them more effectively. It's impossible to learn properly if the material isn't presented in a way that resonates with the way your mind works. You just can't 'hear' it, pick it up or grasp it. Wires then get crossed and the data simply isn't processed. Many children are seriously disadvantaged if learning materials and environments don't speak to them. You may even have been a child like that yourself. If so, you could easily have been left with the false impression that you are a poor learner just because you couldn't get a handle on the lessons being taught. Identifying your own learning style can be like finding the hidden key to the treasure room of knowledge.

The signs of the zodiac are divided into four groups by element:

> The fire signs: Aries, Leo and Sagittarius
> The earth signs: Taurus, Virgo and Capricorn
> The air signs: Gemini, Libra and Aquarius
> The water signs: Cancer, Scorpio and Pisces

Your Mercury will therefore belong to one of the four elements, depending on which sign it is in. Your Mercury can only be in one of three signs – the same sign as your Sun, the one before or the one after. This means that each sign has one learning style that is never natural to it. For Aries, this is the air style.

Mercury in each of the elements has a distinctive way of

operating. I've given the following names to the learning and communicating styles of Mercury through the elements. Mercury in fire – active imaginative; Mercury in earth – practical; Mercury in air – logical; and Mercury in water – impressionable.

Mercury in Fire: Active Imaginative

Your mind is wide open to the excitement of fresh ideas. It responds to action and to the creative possibilities of new situations. Drama, games and storytelling are excellent ways for you to learn. You love to have fun and play with ideas. Any material to be learned has to have some significance for you personally, or add to your self-esteem, otherwise you rapidly lose interest. You learn by acting out the new information, either physically or in your imagination. The most efficient way of succeeding in any goal is to make first a mental picture of your having achieved it. This is called mental rehearsal and is used by many top sportsmen and women as a technique to help improve their performance. You do this spontaneously, as your imagination is your greatest mental asset. You can run through future scenarios in your mind's eye and see, instantly, where a particular piece of information or situation could lead and spot possibilities that other people couldn't even begin to dream of. You are brilliant at coming up with flashes of inspiration for creative breakthroughs and crisis management.

Mercury in Earth: Practical

Endless presentations of feelings, theories and possibilities can make your eyes glaze over and your brain ache to shut down. What really turns you on is trying out these theories and possibilities to see if they work in practice. If they don't, you'll tend to classify them 'of no further interest'. Emotionally charged information is at best a puzzling non-starter and at worst an irritating turn-off. Practical demonstrations, tried and tested facts and working models fascinate you. Hands-on learning, where you can see how a process functions from start to finish, especially if it leads to some useful material end-product, is right up your street. It's important to allow yourself plenty of time when you are learning, writing or thinking out what to say, otherwise you can feel rushed and out of control, never pleasant sensations for earth signs. Your special skill is in coming up with effective solutions to practical problems and in formulating long-range plans that bring concrete, measurable results.

Mercury in Air: Logical

You love learning about, and playing with, ideas, theories and principles. Often you do this best by arguing or bouncing ideas off other people, or by writing down your thoughts. Your special gift is in your ability to stand back and work out the patterns of relationship between people or things. You much prefer it when facts are presented to you logically and unemotionally and have very little time for the irrational, uncertainty or for personal opinions. You do, though, tend to have plenty of those kinds of views yourself, only you call them logical conclusions. Whether a fact is useful or not is less important than whether it fits into your mental map of how the world operates. If facts don't fit in, you'll either ignore them, find a way of making them fit, or, occasionally, make a grand leap to a new, upgraded theory. Yours is the mind of the scientist or chess player. You make a brilliant planner because you can be detached enough to take an overview of the entire situation.

Mercury in Water: Impressionable

Your mind is sensitive to atmospheres and emotional undertones and to the context in which information is presented. Plain facts and figures can often leave you cold and even intimidated. You can take things too personally and read between the lines for what you believe is really being said or taught. If you don't feel emotionally safe, you can be cautious about revealing your true thoughts. It may be hard, or even impossible, for you to learn properly in what you sense is a hostile environment. You are excellent at impression management. Like a skilful artist painting a picture, you can influence others to think what you'd like them to by using suggestive gestures or pauses and intonations. People with Mercury in water signs are often seriously disadvantaged by left-brain schooling methods that are too rigidly structured for them. You take in information best through pictures or images, so that you get a 'feel' for the material and can make an emotional bond with it, in the same way you connect with people. In emotionally supportive situations where there is a rapport between you and your instructors, or your learning material, you are able just to drink in and absorb circulating knowledge without conscious effort, sometimes not even being clear about how or why you know certain things.

Finding Your Mercury Sign

If you don't yet know your Mercury sign, you might like to see if you can guess what it is from the descriptions below before checking it out in the tables on pp. 112–14.

Sun in Aries with Mercury in Aries

Kingsley Amis	Victoria Beckham	Vincent van Gogh
Graham Norton	Rev. Ian Paisley	Ruby Wax

Controversy, conflict and competition grab your attention. Your brain works best in the presence of excitement and action. Life for you is not a spectator sport. You prefer ideas that are the mental equivalent of throwing down the gauntlet. Watching someone with this combination beat down a salesman over the price of a used car is viewing verbal combat at its most audacious and cut-throat. Some of you, like Kingsley Amis, can be deliberately provocative. He would say things like 'If you shut all the hospitals in London, we could have two Trident submarines. Just think . . .'.

Facts and logic alone cut little ice with you. Dry and lifeless theories leave you cold. If information has no power to engage your imagination or to move you to action, it's of marginal interest and you'll quickly find something more upbeat and exciting to occupy your mind. You can come out with some pretty blistering off-the-cuff comments and you tend to blurt things out without thinking them through, often things that would have been best left unvoiced. It is all too easy for you to take what is being said or written as a potential attack and to retaliate aggressively. Sometimes your temper can get the better of you, leading to impulsive acts that you later regret. Vincent van Gogh once threatened fellow painter Gauguin with a razor, then cut off part of his own ear in remorse.

You are a rousing speaker, inspiring people to action and to follow whatever cause you are currently espousing. The Rev. Ian Paisley, the militant Northern Ireland politician, rarely lets an opportunity pass to insult the opposition and rouse his followers to righteous indignation. As part of a team, you are a brilliant brainstormer and have the mental courage to put forward daring suggestions that might have more conservative members trembling in their socks.

Sun in Aries with Mercury in Taurus

Karen Blixen	Isambard Kingdom Brunel	Ram Dass
Spike Milligan	Claudia Cardinale	Valerie Singleton

Your attention is drawn to anything that you believe will lead towards peace and stability and which gives you sensual pleasure. Spiritual teacher Ram Dass speaks disarmingly about his time in India as a holy man pretending for the sake of devotees that his mind was above lowly pleasures, all the while thinking about, and enjoying when he could, delicious food and sweets, and other fleshly delights. You have an eye for beauty, an ear for music and a mind focused on practicalities. Speaking plainly, you say it as it is without frills or flattery.

You need time, and plenty of it, to take in, check out and assimilate new ideas and information. It is helpful if you are allowed, and allow yourself, to savour anything new with the senses for a while until it becomes familiar. The Arien low threshold of boredom does not apply to your mental resources and processes. Once you have accepted an idea that you have so carefully made your own, and closed your mind around it, you tend to remain loyal, defending your stance firmly against any opposing thought. You are willing to fight for your ideas if need be and invest a great deal of effort into putting them across forcefully. This can be a great advantage in giving you the persistence to follow through on projects and to achieve something substantial. However, if it gets to the point where you reject out of hand any ideas other than your own, you can become inflexible. At worst this can lead to belligerent bigotry. For you, there is nothing contradictory in the notion of making war with words for the sake of peace.

Sun in Aries with Mercury in Pisces

| Maya Angelou | Jeffrey Archer | Rory Bremner |
| Richard Dawkins | Doris Day | Michael Parkinson |

You are highly attuned to emotional atmospheres. Being well-nigh psychic, you can pick up on thoughts that are 'in the air' and may find it difficult to distinguish clear boundaries between what you and other people are thinking. Negative circulating thoughts can be for you a form of psychic contamination against which you need to learn to protect yourself. The biologist Richard Dawkins writes about contagious ideas called 'memes' that leap from brain to brain, competing for attention. That sounds like an excellent insider's description of an Aries Sun with Mercury in Pisces. Being so impressionable, you are sensitive and easily hurt, and occasionally prone to bouts of self-pity. You are also quick to notice other people's suffering and longings for life to be better. By acting on these insights, you can make a great contribution to helping others, but you first need to be sure that you're not responding to emotional manipulation and becoming needlessly guilty.

Being what is called a right-brain learner, mainstream academic teaching styles that concentrate on logic and learning by rote rarely work in your favour. You may often seem dreamy and absent-minded and, being highly imaginative, poetic and romantic, the harsh facts of real life may bruise your fantasies. Jeffrey Archer's wife says that he is the master of inaccurate précis. Children with this combination often need to be taught, gently but firmly, the difference between fact and fiction.

You can often be the mouthpiece for saying out loud what everybody else is feeling just below the surface of consciousness. Being a wonderful impressionist, able to conjure up verbal pictures of what you sense people want to hear rather than necessarily the precise and literal truth, you could do well in the media, advertising or the arts.

NINE

Venus — At Your Pleasure

♀ THE GLYPH FOR VENUS IS MADE UP OF THE CIRCLE OF ETERNITY on top of the cross of matter. Esoterically this represents love, which is a quality of the divine, revealed on earth through personal choice. The saying 'One man's meat is another man's poison' couldn't be more relevant when it comes to what we love. It is a mystery why we find one thing attractive and another unattractive, or even repulsive. Looking at the sign, aspects and house of your Venus can't give any explanation of this mystery, but it can give some clear indications of what it is that you value and find desirable. This can be quite different from what current fashion tells you you should like. For example, many people are strongly turned on by voluptuous bodies but the media constantly shows images of near-anorexics as the desirable ideal. If you ignore what you, personally, find beautiful and try to be, or to love, what at heart leaves you cold, you are setting yourself up for unnecessary pain and dissatisfaction. Being true to your Venus sign, even if other people think you are strange, brings joy and pleasure. It also builds up your self-esteem because it grounds you solidly in your own personal values. This, in turn, makes you much more attractive to others. Not only that, it improves your relationships immeasurably, because you are living authentically and not betraying yourself by trying to prove your worth to others by being something you are not.

Glittering Venus, the brightest planet in the heavens, was named after the goddess of love, war and victory. Earlier names for her were Aphrodite, Innana and Ishtar. She was beautiful, self-willed and self-indulgent but was also skilled in all the arts of civilisation.

Your Venus sign shows what you desire and would like to possess, not only in relationships but also in all aspects of your taste, from clothes and culture to hobbies and hobby-horses. It identifies how and where you can be charming and seductive and skilful at creating your own type of beauty yourself. It also describes your style of attracting partners and the kind of people that turn you on. When your Venus is activated you feel powerful, desirable and wonderfully, wickedly indulged and indulgent. When it is not, even if someone has all the right credentials to make a good match, the relationship will always lack that certain something. If you don't take the chance to express your Venus to a good enough degree somewhere in your life, you miss out woefully on delight and happiness.

Morning Star, Evening Star

Venus appears in the sky either in the morning or in the evening. The ancients launched their attacks when Venus became a morning star, believing that she was then in her warrior-goddess role, releasing aggressive energy for victory in battle. If you're a morning-star person, you're likely to be impulsive, self-willed and idealistic, prepared to hold out until you find the partner who is just right for you.

Relationships and business dealings of morning-star Venus people are said to prosper best whenever Venus in the sky is a morning star. If you are an early bird, you can check this out. At these times Venus can be seen in the eastern sky before the Sun has risen.

The name for Venus as an evening star is Hesperus and it was then, traditionally, said to be sacred to lovers. Evening-star people tend to be easy-going and are open to negotiation, conciliation and making peace. If you are an evening-star Venus person, your best times in relationship and business affairs are said to be when Venus can be seen, jewel-like, in the western sky after the Sun has set.

Because the orbit of Venus is so close to the Sun, your Venus can only be in one of five signs. You have a morning-star Venus if your Venus is in one of the two signs that come before your Sun sign in the zodiac. You have an evening-star Venus if your Venus is in either of the two signs that follow your Sun sign. If you have Venus in the same sign as your Sun, you could be either, depending on whether your Venus is ahead of or behind your Sun. (You can find out which at the author's website www.janeridderpatrick.com.)

If you don't yet know your Venus sign, you might like to read through all of the following descriptions and see if you can guess what it is. You can find out for sure on pp. 115–18.

At the beginning of each section are the names of some well-known Ariens with that particular Venus sign. You can find out more about them in Chapter Ten, Famous Aries Birthdays.

Sun in Aries with Venus in Aries

Joan Bakewell   Doris Day   Robert Downey Jr
Harry Houdini   Steve McQueen   Ruby Wax

You love the adrenalin rush of risk and could even go out of your way to attract danger. Houdini made a career out of spectacular escapes from death-defying situations. Favourites were being suspended in a straitjacket from a high building or jumping manacled off a bridge. Passionate and impulsive, you can fall head over heels in love, and then out of it again, with remarkable speed. While it is certainly not impossible for you to stay constant, many people with this combination have at some time been overcome by the raging fires of desire and made a rash move in the romance department only to have their fingers badly burnt. It's all too easy for you to confuse your powerful urge to conquer with love. You tend to be attracted to strong, feisty, independent types who may even be rather brash and abrasive – as you can be yourself. Man or woman, you can come on strong: once your hunting instinct is roused, you're impatient to lay claim to the object of your affections now, this very instant. With little subtlety or bashfulness, but naivety in buckets, you'll plunge straight in on an overwhelming impulse, giving no thought for the practicalities of the situation. One such Aries admirer wooed his lady with the hot-breathed confession that he wanted to come round, smash her door down and take her in the hallway. The fact that they were neighbours and married, but to other people, was brushed aside as a trifle. The thrill of the chase turns you on and the harder the prize is to win, the better you like it. But if the tables are turned and you become the hunted, you're liable to do a runner.

Sun in Aries with Venus in Taurus

Jane Asher	Warren Beatty	Charlie Chaplin
Andrew Lloyd	Debbie Reynolds	Penelope Keith
Webber		

Sun in Aries with Venus in Taurus combines the romantic dash and daring of Aries with the slow sensuality of Taurus. While you're certainly not immune to the impulsive crushes that dramatise, and sometimes booby trap, the love lives of Ariens, it may take you some considerable time to become seriously involved in a committed relationship. As you are willing to fight for what you love, heaven help anyone who tries to muscle in on your patch. You can be more than a little possessive about what you consider is your property, and that includes those that you love.

You can be deeply appreciative of nature so a garden or easy access to the countryside in all its seasonal glory is important to you. Good food, music, art and the finer things in life give you immense satisfaction. Life without quality sex would be almost unimaginable to you. You're old-fashioned at heart and like to spoil your loved ones with tangible demonstrations of affection: gifts, flowers and chocolates as well as back rubs and bearhugs. A reliable, trustworthy partner suits you best, one who you know will always be there for you. Your need for continuity can mean you stay in a relationship out of habit when love has long since vanished.

You are usually more sensible and careful with your cash than other Ariens. Money means a lot to you, both for the security it brings and the comforting luxuries it buys, the foremost among those being a solid, comfortable home, fully paid up. Lasting happiness comes when you cultivate the serene outlook of Chaplin's best-loved character 'the Little Tramp', who stays placid and optimistic no matter what chaos threatens to engulf him.

Sun in Aries with Venus in Gemini

Jeffrey Archer	Bette Davis	Omar Sharif
Dudley Moore	Emma Thompson	Russell Crowe

Sexually souped-up Aries with a restless Gemini Venus could mean your attention span in the romance stakes tends to be short. The tug of novelty and the enticement of new conquests can be compelling. Your sunny charm and way with words can make you an outrageous flirt, with some dazzlingly cheeky come-ons. This makes it quite a challenge for you to stay at heel in any committed relationship, but you can do it if you try. Any leash that a partner tries to keep you on needs to be long and elastic.

Variety is your spice in life and you may be skilled in two fields; heart-throb actor Omar Sharif is also a world-class bridge player; Dudley Moore was a comedian and musician, while Jeffrey Archer is an author and politician. It's easy for you to get on with just about everybody. While you're happy to share all the superficial details about yourself and are intensely curious about the lives of others, you can't stand being pinned down either emotionally or physically. If things start to get heavy, you'll begin to squirm and evade and check out the exits. Boredom is your worst nightmare, so it's essential that you have a lively-minded partner who stimulates what's between your ears as well as elsewhere. The sparky exchange of words turns you on so you need plenty of response and verbal banter from your partner. As you love making deals and have a sharp eye for business potential, if you turn your mind to it, you should find no difficulty in channelling money your way. Unfortunately you're also impulsive and extravagant so it's often a case of easy come, easy go.

Sun in Aries with Venus in Aquarius

Robbie Coltrane	Chris Evans	Aretha Franklin
Elton John	Erica Jong	Gloria Steinem

Cool, friendly companionship is often more to your liking than hot, steamy passion. Powerful emotions, especially of the dark and dangerous kind, and too much intimacy can make you want to run for cover. Your natural emotional reserve can sometimes be mistaken for aloofness, but you are far from cold. Friends mean a great deal to you. You can go to extraordinary lengths to help if they are ever in trouble. Without them you can feel quite isolated because you're often out of step with what most so-called normal people think and desire. Being part of a group that's on your wavelength, preferably fighting for something that betters the human condition, can bring you happiness and opportunities for lasting love. You've an unselfish streak when it comes to money and could even be attracted to fundraising for good causes. For any long-lasting commitment, a like-minded partner who shares your ideas and ideals is a must.

Your pleasures and tastes can be non-conformist and your dress sense quite outrageous. Elton John's party frocks are more off-the-wall than off-the-peg. You may get a kick out of challenging tradition and can get up to some wildly unconventional behaviour when the mood strikes. There is part of you that doesn't give a fig what others think and you sometimes delight in shocking just for the sheer hell of it. Some Ariens with Venus in Aquarius are emotionally detached when it comes to sex, notching up conquests on the bedposts, their hearts untouched, like Erica Jong's character from *Fear of Flying*, a woman in search of her ultimate sexual experience – 'the zipless f**k'. Others, once committed, are so highly principled that they would almost rather die than deceive.

Sun in Aries with Venus in Pisces

Victoria Beckham	Vincent van Gogh	Hugh Hefner
Ewan McGregor	Diana Ross	Dusty Springfield

You're in love with love and long for the fusion of hearts and perfect bliss in the arms of a lover. Because of your gentleness, openness and sensitivity, you need to be selective about who you allow into your intimate circle, as you can be easily hurt and taken advantage of. Fleetingly, you can fall in love with, or see something divine in, just about everyone you meet. You may need to check a tendency to confuse pity and sympathy with love or to be led (or lead others!) astray with a good seductive line or hard-luck story. You can create shimmering illusions of glamour and have a glorious knack of acting out other people's fantasies, but can sometimes feel guilty about asking for what you want and end up feeling resentful. Alternatively you could try to sculpt your partner to suit your dreams, like Hugh Hefner, founder of *Playboy* magazine, who insisted for a while that all the women in his personal harem be – or become – blonde.

You're capable of devoted, sometimes self-sacrificial,

and deeply spiritual love. You're searching for your prince or princess who will make your fantasies come true, save you from suffering and magic away all your inadequacies and protect you from any contact with harsh reality — or to be that person yourself. When you believe you've found your perfect match, you can be totally besotted. However, it's important to adjust a little to reality, otherwise you run the risk of feeling bitterly let down and disappointed when you find that your partner snores, gets grumpy or wants their own way, just like any other normal, imperfect human being.

TEN

Famous Aries Birthdays

FIND OUT WHO SHARES YOUR MOON, MERCURY AND VENUS SIGNS, and any challenging Sun aspects, and see what they have done with the material they were born with. Notice how often it is not just the personalities of the people themselves but the roles of actors, characters of authors and works of artists that reflect their astrological make-up. In reading standard biographies, I've been constantly astounded – and, of course, delighted – at how often phrases used to describe individuals could have been lifted straight from their astrological profiles. Check it out yourself!

A few people below have been given a choice of two Moons. This is because the Moon changed sign on the day that they were born and no birth time was available. You may be able to guess which one is correct if you read the descriptions of the Moon signs in Chapter Seven.

21 March
1685: Johann Sebastian Bach, one of the world's greatest composers
Sun aspects: Pluto
Moon: Aquarius or Pisces   Mercury: Pisces   Venus: Pisces

22 March
1948: Andrew Lloyd Webber, composer of *Evita* and *Cats*
Sun aspects: Uranus, Neptune
Moon: Leo   Mercury: Pisces   Venus: Taurus

23 March
1929: Sir Roger Bannister, the first person to run a mile in under four minutes
Sun aspects: Saturn, Uranus
Moon: Virgo   Mercury: Pisces   Venus: Taurus

24 March
1930: Steve McQueen, actor, *The Great Escape*, *Bullitt*
Sun aspects: Saturn, Uranus
Moon: Aquarius   Mercury: Pisces   Venus: Aries

25 March
1947: Elton John, flamboyant singer and owner of Rocket records
Sun aspects: Neptune
Moon: Taurus   Mercury: Pisces   Venus: Aquarius

26 March
1942: Erica Jong, feminist author of the sexually explicit novel *Fear of Flying*
Sun aspects: Neptune
Moon: Cancer   Mercury: Pisces   Venus: Aquarius

27 March
1845: Wilhelm von Roentgen, German scientist who discovered X-rays
Sun aspects: Uranus
Moon: Scorpio   Mercury: Aries   Venus: Pisces

28 March
1515: Saint Teresa of Avila, who saw visions and reformed the Carmelite Order
Sun aspects: Uranus
Moon: Virgo   Mercury: Aries   Venus: Pisces

29 March
1918: Pearl Bailey, American entertainer and 'ambassador of love' to the UN
Sun aspects: Pluto
Moon: Libra   Mercury: Aries   Venus: Aquarius

30 March
1853: Vincent van Gogh, Dutch painter, missing part of an ear
Sun aspects: none
Moon: Sagittarius   Mercury: Aries   Venus: Pisces

31 March
1971: Ewan McGregor, actor, *Trainspotting*, *Star Wars* and *Moulin Rouge*
Sun aspects: Uranus
Moon: Gemini   Mercury: Aries   Venus: Pisces

1 April
1815: Otto von Bismarck, the 'man of blood and iron' who unified Germany
Sun aspects: none
Moon: Capricorn   Mercury: Pisces   Venus: Taurus

2 April
1805: Hans Christian Andersen, writer of fairytales, such as *The Emperor's New Clothes*
Sun aspects: Saturn, Uranus
Moon: Taurus   Mercury: Aries   Venus: Pisces

3 April
1922: Doris Day, American actress with girl-next-door appeal, *Pillow Talk*
Sun aspects: Saturn, Pluto
Moon: Gemini   Mercury: Pisces   Venus: Aries

4 April
1928: Maya Angelou, American writer, *I Know Why the Caged Bird Sings*
Sun aspects: Pluto
Moon: Libra   Mercury: Pisces   Venus: Pisces

5 April
1908: Bette Davis, actress, *Dangerous*, *Jezebel*
Sun aspects: Uranus, Neptune
Moon: Gemini   Mercury: Pisces   Venus: Gemini

6 April
1926 Rev. Ian Paisley, militant Northern Irish Protestant leader
Sun aspects: Pluto
Moon: Capricorn   Mercury: Aries   Venus: Pisces

7 April
1770: William Wordsworth, poet, famous for 'Daffodils'
Sun aspects: Saturn, Pluto
Moon: Virgo   Mercury: Pisces   Venus: Aries

8 April
1941: Vivienne Westwood, avant-garde fashion designer
Sun aspects: none
Moon: Leo   Mercury: Pisces   Venus: Aries

9 April
1806: Isambard Kingdom Brunel, outstanding Victorian engineer, builder of first steamship to cross the Atlantic
Sun aspects: Saturn, Uranus
Moon: Sagittarius   Mercury: Taurus   Venus: Pisces

10 April
1755: Samuel Hahnemann, founder of homoeopathy
Sun aspects: Saturn
Moon: Aries   Mercury: Aries   Venus: Pisces

11 April
1963: June and Jennifer Gibbons, the silent twins who spoke only their own secret language and were sent to Broadmoor prison for arson and vandalism
Sun aspects: none
Moon: Scorpio   Mercury: Taurus   Venus: Pisces

12 April
1941: Booby Moore, footballer who led England to victory in the 1966 World Cup
Sun aspects: none
Moon: Libra   Mercury: Pisces   Venus: Aries

13 April
1937: Edward Fox, actor, *The Day of the Jackal*
Sun aspects: Pluto
Moon: Taurus or Gemini   Mercury: Taurus   Venus: Taurus

14 April
1961: Robert Carlyle, actor, *Trainspotting* and *The Full Monty*
Sun aspects: Saturn
Moon: Aries   Mercury: Aries   Venus: Aries

15 April
1940: Jeffrey Archer, English politician and bestselling novelist, jailed for perjury
Sun aspects: Saturn, Pluto
Moon: Cancer   Mercury: Pisces   Venus: Gemini

16 April
1867: Wilbur Wright, aviation pioneer, making the first sustained air flight in 1903
Sun aspects: none
Moon: Aquarius   Mercury: Pisces   Venus: Taurus

17 April

1946: Clare Francis, solo round-the-world yachtswoman
Sun aspects: Saturn
Moon: Scorpio   Mercury: Aries   Venus: Taurus

18 April

1959: Susan Faludi, feminist writer specialising in women's image in the media
Sun aspects: Neptune
Moon: Leo   Mercury: Aries   Venus: Gemini

19 April

1953: Ruby Wax, irrepressibly cheeky TV interviewer and comedian
Sun aspects: Saturn, Neptune
Moon: Cancer   Mercury: Aries   Venus: Aries

Other Aries people mentioned in this book

Kingsley Amis, writer, *Lucky Jim* ☆ Jane Asher, actress and cookery writer ☆ Joan Bakewell, TV presenter once called 'the thinking man's crumpet' ☆ Warren Beatty, sultry actor, *Shampoo* ☆ Victoria Beckham, former Spice Girl married to footballer David Beckham ☆ Karen Blixen, writer, *Out of Africa* ☆ Dirk Bogarde, actor, *Death in Venice* ☆ William Booth, founder of the Salvation Army ☆ Marlon Brando, actor, *The Godfather* ☆ Rory Bremner, impressionist, *Spitting Image* ☆ Claudia Cardinale, curvaceous Italian actress, *The Leopard* ☆ Giacomo Casanova, sexual adventurer ☆ Richard Chamberlain, actor, *Dr Kildare* ☆ Charlie Chaplin, actor, *City Lights* ☆ Julie Christie, actress, *Doctor Zhivago* ☆ Robbie Coltrane, actor, *Cracker*, Hagrid in *Harry Potter* ☆ Joan Crawford, actress, *What Ever Happened to Baby Jane?* ☆ Russell Crowe, actor, *Gladiator*, *A Beautiful Mind* ☆ Erich von Daniken, controversial alien-theory writer, *Chariots of the Gods* ☆ Ram

Dass, pop guru, 'be here now' ☆ Richard Dawkins, biologist, *The Selfish Gene* ☆ Robert Downey Jr, actor, who played fellow Arien Charlie in *Chaplin* ☆ Ian Duncan Smith, Conservative party leader ☆ Chris Evans, red-haired radio and TV presenter, chairman of the Ginger Media Group ☆ Marilyn Ferguson, futurist, *The Aquarian Conspiracy* ☆ Betty Ford, former US First Lady ☆ Viktor Frankl, Auschwitz survivor and founder of logotherapy, the psychology of meaning ☆ Aretha Franklin, singer, *Ain't No Way* ☆ Erich Fromm, psychologist, *The Art of Loving*, *The Anatomy of Human Destructiveness* ☆ David Frost, TV host, *That Was The Week That Was* ☆ William Hague, former Conservative party leader ☆ Emmylou Harris, singer, 'Sweet Dreams' ☆ Rolf Harris, artist and TV presenter ☆ Hugh Hefner, publisher of *Playboy* magazine ☆ Harry Houdini, escapologist, magician and exposer of phoney mediums ☆ Olivia Hussey, actress, *Death on the Nile* ☆ Penelope Keith, actress, *The Good Life* ☆ Kitty Kelley, writer of muck-raking unauthorised biographies ☆ Rodney King, victim of police crime ☆ James Lovell, astronaut ☆ Ali MacGraw, actress, *Love Story* ☆ John Major, former British Prime Minister ☆ Chico Marx, one of the Marx Brothers comedians ☆ Spike Milligan, comedian, *The Goon Show* ☆ Mistinguett, glamorous French queen of the music halls ☆ Dudley Moore, comedian and musician, *Arthur* ☆ John Pierpoint Morgan, American banker, financier and art collector ☆ Piers Morgan, tabloid newspaper editor ☆ William Morris, artist and craftsman ☆ Eddie Murphy, actor, *The Nutty Professor* ☆ Elliot Ness, head of The Untouchables, a supposedly incorruptible US law enforcement agency ☆ Graham Norton, comedian and cheeky TV presenter ☆ Sarah Jessica Parker, actress, *Sex and the City* ☆ Michael Parkinson, TV talk-show host ☆ Gregory Peck, actor, *To Kill a Mockingbird* ☆ Paloma Picasso, perfumier and daughter of the painter Pablo Picasso ☆ Diana Ross, singer, 'Endless Love' ☆ Omar Sharif, actor, *Doctor Zhivago* ☆ Simone Signoret, actress,

Ship of Fools ☆ Valerie Singleton, *Blue Peter* children's TV presenter ☆ Dusty Springfield, singer, 'I Only Want to be With You' ☆ Gloria Steinem, feminist writer and publisher *Ms Magazine* ☆ Annie Sullivan, teacher of Helen Keller ☆ Gloria Swanson, 'queen of the screen' actress, *Sunset Boulevard* ☆ Paul Theroux, writer, *Kingdom by the Sea* ☆ Emma Thompson, actress, *Much Ado About Nothing* ☆ Kenneth Tynan, theatre critic ☆ Peter Ustinov, actor, dramatist and film director, *Evil Under the Sun* ☆ James D. Watson, co-discoverer of the structure of DNA ☆ Tennessee Williams, playwright, *Cat on a Hot Tin Roof*

ELEVEN

Finding Your Sun, Moon, Mercury and Venus Signs

ALL OF THE ASTROLOGICAL DATA IN THIS BOOK WAS CALCULATED by Astrolabe, who also supply a wide range of astrological software. I am most grateful for their help and generosity.

ASTROLABE, PO Box 1750, Brewster, MA 02631, USA www.alabe.com

PLEASE NOTE THAT ALL OF THE TIMES GIVEN ARE IN GREENWICH MEAN TIME (GMT). If you were born during British Summer Time (BST) you will need to subtract one hour from your birth time to convert it to GMT. If you were born outside of the British Isles, find the time zone of your place of birth and the number of hours it is different from GMT. Add the difference in hours if you were born west of the UK, and subtract the difference if you were born east of the UK to convert your birth time to GMT.

Your Sun Sign

Check your year of birth, and if you were born between the dates and times given the Sun was in Aries when you were born – confirming that you're an Arien. If you were born before the time on the date that Aries begins in your year, you are a Piscean. If you were born after the time on the date Aries ends in your year, you are a Taurean.

Your Moon Sign

The Moon changes sign every two and a half days. To find your Moon sign, first find your year of birth. You will notice that in each year box there are three columns.

The second column shows the day of the month that the Moon changed sign, while the first column gives the abbreviation for the sign that the Moon entered on that date.

In the middle column, the month has been omitted, so that the dates run from, for example, 20 to 31 (of March) and then from 1 to 19 (of April).

In the third column, after the star, the time that the Moon changed sign on that day is given.

Look down the middle column of your year box to find your date of birth. If your birth date is given, look to the third column to find the time that the Moon changed sign. If you were born after that time, your Moon sign is given in the first column next to your birth date. If you were born before that time, your Moon sign is the one above the one next to your birth date.

If your birth date is not given, find the closest date before it. The sign shown next to that date is your Moon sign.

If you were born on a day that the Moon changed signs and you do not know your time of birth, try out both of that day's Moon signs and feel which one fits you best.

The abbreviations for the signs are as follows:

Aries – Ari   Taurus – Tau   Gemini – Gem   Cancer – Can
Leo – Leo   Virgo – Vir   Libra – Lib   Scorpio – Sco
Sagittarius – Sag Capricorn – Cap   Aquarius – Aqu   Pisces – Pis

Your Mercury Sign

Find your year of birth and then the column in which your birthday falls. Look up to the top of the column to find your Mercury sign. You will see that some dates appear twice. This is because Mercury changed sign that day. If your birthday falls on one of these dates, try out both Mercury signs and see which one fits you best. If you know your birth time, you can find out for sure which Mercury sign is yours on my website – www.janeridderpatrick.com.

Your Venus Sign

Find your year of birth and then the column in which your birthday falls. Look up to the top of the column to find your Venus sign. Some dates have two possible signs. That's because Venus changed signs that day. Try them both out and see which fits you best. If the year you are interested in doesn't appear in the tables, or you have Venus in the same sign as your Sun and want to know whether you have a morning or evening star Venus, you can find the information on my website – www.janeridderpatrick.com.

♈ Aries Sun Tables ☉

YEAR	ARIES BEGINS	ARIES ENDS
1930	21 Mar at 08.29	20 Apr at 20.05
1931	21 Mar at 14.06	21 Apr at 01.39
1932	20 Mar at 19.53	20 Apr at 07.28
1933	21 Mar at 01.43	20 Apr at 13.18
1934	21 Mar at 07.28	20 Apr at 19.00
1935	21 Mar at 13.17	21 Apr at 00.50
1936	20 Mar at 18.57	20 Apr at 06.31
1937	21 Mar at 00.45	20 Apr at 12.19
1938	21 Mar at 06.43	20 Apr at 18.14
1939	21 Mar at 12.28	20 Apr at 23.55
1940	20 Mar at 18.23	20 Apr at 05.51
1941	21 Mar at 00.20	20 Apr at 11.50
1942	21 Mar at 06.10	20 Apr at 17.39
1943	21 Mar at 12.02	20 Apr at 23.31
1944	20 Mar at 17.48	20 Apr at 05.17
1945	20 Mar at 23.37	20 Apr at 11.06
1946	21 Mar at 05.32	20 Apr at 17.02
1947	21 Mar at 11.12	20 Apr at 22.39
1948	20 Mar at 16.56	20 Apr at 04.24
1949	20 Mar at 22.48	20 Apr at 10.17
1950	21 Mar at 04.35	20 Apr at 15.59
1951	21 Mar at 10.25	20 Apr at 21.48
1952	20 Mar at 16.13	20 Apr at 03.36
1953	20 Mar at 22.00	20 Apr at 09.25
1954	21 Mar at 03.53	20 Apr at 15.19
1955	21 Mar at 09.35	20 Apr at 20.57
1956	20 Mar at 15.20	20 Apr at 02.43
1957	20 Mar at 21.16	20 Apr at 08.41
1958	21 Mar at 03.05	20 Apr at 14.27
1959	21 Mar at 08.54	20 Apr at 20.16
1960	20 Mar at 14.42	20 Apr at 02.05
1961	20 Mar at 20.32	20 Apr at 07.55
1962	21 Mar at 02.29	20 Apr at 13.50
1963	21 Mar at 08.19	20 Apr at 19.36

YEAR	ARIES BEGINS	ARIES ENDS
1964	20 Mar at 14.09	20 Apr at 01.27
1965	20 Mar at 20.04	20 Apr at 07.26
1966	21 Mar at 01.53	20 Apr at 13.11
1967	21 Mar at 07.36	20 Apr at 18.55
1968	20 Mar at 13.22	20 Apr at 00.41
1969	20 Mar at 19.08	20 Apr at 06.26
1970	21 Mar at 00.56	20 Apr at 12.14
1971	21 Mar at 06.38	20 Apr at 17.54
1972	20 Mar at 12.21	19 Apr at 23.37
1973	20 Mar at 18.12	20 Apr at 05.30
1974	21 Mar at 00.06	20 Apr at 11.18
1975	21 Mar at 05.56	20 Apr at 17.07
1976	20 Mar at 11.49	19 Apr at 23.03
1977	20 Mar at 17.42	20 Apr at 04.57
1978	20 Mar at 23.33	20 Apr at 10.49
1979	21 Mar at 05.22	20 Apr at 16.35
1980	20 Mar at 11.09	19 Apr at 22.22
1981	20 Mar at 17.02	20 Apr at 04.18
1982	20 Mar at 22.55	20 Apr at 10.07
1983	21 Mar at 04.38	20 Apr at 15.50
1984	20 Mar at 10.24	19 Apr at 21.38
1985	20 Mar at 16.13	20 Apr at 03.25
1986	20 Mar at 22.02	20 Apr at 09.12
1987	21 Mar at 03.52	20 Apr at 14.57
1988	20 Mar at 09.38	19 Apr at 20.44
1989	20 Mar at 15.28	20 Apr at 02.39
1990	20 Mar at 21.19	20 Apr at 08.26
1991	21 Mar at 03.02	20 Apr at 14.08
1992	20 Mar at 08.48	19 Apr at 19.56
1993	20 Mar at 14.40	20 Apr at 01.49
1994	20 Mar at 20.28	20 Apr at 07.36
1995	21 Mar at 02.14	20 Apr at 13.21
1996	20 Mar at 08.03	19 Apr at 19.09
1997	20 Mar at 13.54	20 Apr at 01.02
1998	20 Mar at 19.54	20 Apr at 06.56
1999	21 Mar at 01.45	20 Apr at 12.45
2000	20 Mar at 07.35	19 Apr at 18.39

♈ Aries – Finding Your Moon Sign ☽

1930		
Cap	22	*01:40
Aqu	24	*14:04
Pis	27	*02:23
Ari	29	*12:59
Tau	31	*21:22
Gem	3	*03:41
Can	5	*08:10
Leo	7	*11:08
Vir	9	*13:10
Lib	11	*15:17
Sco	13	*18:44
Sag	16	*00:50
Cap	18	*10:07

1931		
Tau	22	*00:43
Gem	24	*11:18
Can	26	*19:04
Leo	28	*23:27
Vir	31	*00:56
Lib	2	*00:49
Sco	4	*00:51
Sag	6	*02:53
Cap	8	*08:21
Aqu	10	*17:40
Pis	13	*05:48
Ari	15	*18:47
Tau	18	*06:50

1932		
Vir	20	*09:17
Lib	22	*09:56
Sco	24	*09:35
Sag	26	*10:07
Cap	28	*13:08
Aqu	30	*19:30
Pis	2	*05:04
Ari	4	*16:53
Tau	7	*05:43
Gem	9	*18:26
Can	12	*05:46
Leo	14	*14:20
Vir	16	*19:20
Lib	18	*20:59

1933		
Aqu	21	*04:39
Pis	23	*10:16
Ari	25	*17:49
Tau	28	*03:32
Gem	30	*15:13
Can	2	*03:49
Leo	4	*15:15
Vir	6	*23:31
Lib	9	*03:59
Sco	11	*05:31
Sag	13	*05:51
Cap	15	*06:53
Aqu	17	*10:03
Pis	19	*15:54

1934		
Gem	20	*10:52
Can	22	*22:13
Leo	25	*11:02
Vir	27	*22:43
Lib	30	*07:36
Sco	1	*13:34
Sag	3	*17:36
Cap	5	*20:45
Aqu	7	*23:42
Pis	10	*02:52
Ari	12	*06:40
Tau	14	*11:56
Gem	16	*19:41
Can	19	*06:26

♈ Aries – Finding Your Moon Sign ☽

1935			1936			1937			1938			1939		
Lib	20	*08:07	Pis	21	*00:57	Leo	21	*19:35	Sag	21	*07:01	Ari	21	*02:40
Sco	22	*18:44	Ari	23	*00:31	Vir	24	*02:44	Cap	23	*19:31	Tau	23	*11:57
Sag	25	*03:23	Tau	24	*23:38	Lib	26	*11:47	Aqu	26	*07:55	Gem	25	*19:14
Cap	27	*09:47	Gem	27	*00:32	Sco	28	*22:51	Pis	28	*17:51	Can	28	*00:18
Aqu	29	*13:40	Can	29	*04:52	Sag	31	*11:32	Ari	31	*00:32	Leo	30	*03:14
Pis	31	*15:14	Leo	31	*13:04	Cap	3	*00:15	Tau	2	*04:42	Vir	1	*04:38
Ari	2	*15:31	Vir	3	*00:07	Aqu	5	*10:37	Gem	4	*07:33	Lib	3	*05:48
Tau	4	*16:18	Lib	5	*12:30	Pis	7	*16:58	Can	6	*10:07	Sco	5	*08:22
Gem	6	*19:35	Sco	8	*01:04	Ari	9	*19:27	Leo	8	*13:04	Sag	7	*13:48
Can	9	*02:49	Sag	10	*13:02	Tau	11	*19:39	Vir	10	*16:51	Cap	9	*22:47
Leo	11	*13:52	Cap	12	*23:21	Gem	13	*19:34	Lib	12	*22:02	Aqu	12	*10:33
Vir	14	*02:46	Aqu	15	*06:48	Can	15	*21:03	Sco	15	*05:21	Pis	14	*23:04
Lib	16	*15:00	Pis	17	*10:36	Leo	18	*01:12	Sag	17	*15:19	Ari	17	*10:12
Sco	19	*01:08	Ari	19	*11:19							Tau	19	*18:56

99

♈ Aries – Finding Your Moon Sign ☽

1940		
Vir	21	*15:19
Lib	23	*14:47
Sco	25	*14:33
Sag	27	*16:31
Cap	29	*22:00
Aqu	1	*07:13
Pis	3	*19:10
Ari	6	*08:09
Tau	8	*20:38
Gem	11	*07:31
Can	13	*16:03
Leo	15	*21:42
Vir	18	*00:33

1941		
Cap	20	*04:25
Aqu	22	*10:34
Pis	24	*19:30
Ari	27	*06:39
Tau	29	*19:13
Gem	1	*08:06
Can	3	*19:43
Leo	6	*04:25
Vir	8	*09:19
Lib	10	*10:53
Sco	12	*10:31
Sag	14	*10:08
Cap	16	*11:39
Aqu	18	*16:31

1942		
Gem	22	*04:00
Can	24	*16:32
Leo	27	*04:03
Vir	29	*12:35
Lib	31	*17:36
Sco	2	*19:54
Sag	4	*21:04
Cap	6	*22:42
Aqu	9	*01:57
Pis	11	*07:19
Ari	13	*14:49
Tau	16	*00:18
Gem	18	*11:36

1943		
Lib	21	*21:20
Sco	24	*04:22
Sag	26	*09:22
Cap	28	*13:04
Aqu	30	*15:56
Pis	1	*18:26
Ari	3	*21:17
Tau	6	*01:38
Gem	8	*08:42
Can	10	*19:03
Leo	13	*07:39
Vir	15	*19:58
Lib	18	*05:40

1944		
Aqu	20	*04:54
Pis	22	*05:58
Ari	24	*05:41
Tau	26	*06:00
Gem	28	*08:59
Can	30	*15:59
Leo	2	*02:54
Vir	4	*15:48
Lib	7	*04:21
Sco	9	*15:11
Sag	12	*00:01
Cap	14	*06:55
Aqu	16	*11:44
Pis	18	*14:27

♈ Aries — Finding Your Moon Sign ☽

1945		
Can	20	*19:31
Leo	23	*03:32
Vir	25	*14:11
Lib	28	*02:15
Sco	30	*14:49
Sag	2	*03:07
Cap	4	*13:50
Aqu	6	*21:26
Pis	9	*01:08
Ari	11	*01:37
Tau	13	*00:39
Gem	15	*00:32
Can	17	*03:14
Leo	19	*09:53

1946		
Sco	20	*12:05
Sag	23	*00:30
Cap	25	*13:16
Aqu	27	*23:49
Pis	30	*06:25
Ari	1	*09:15
Tau	3	*09:56
Gem	5	*10:25
Can	7	*12:21
Leo	9	*16:37
Vir	11	*23:20
Lib	14	*08:13
Sco	16	*19:03
Sag	19	*07:29

1947		
Pis	20	*06:57
Ari	22	*14:22
Tau	24	*19:28
Gem	26	*23:15
Can	29	*02:25
Leo	31	*05:22
Vir	2	*08:30
Lib	4	*12:40
Sco	6	*18:56
Sag	9	*04:12
Cap	11	*16:08
Aqu	14	*04:50
Pis	16	*15:46
Ari	18	*23:24

1948		
Leo	20	*18:57
Vir	22	*19:42
Lib	24	*20:01
Sco	26	*21:50
Sag	29	*02:47
Cap	31	*11:34
Aqu	2	*23:18
Pis	5	*11:55
Ari	7	*23:27
Tau	10	*08:57
Gem	12	*16:19
Can	14	*21:40
Leo	17	*01:15
Vir	19	*03:30

1949		
Cap	21	*12:05
Aqu	23	*21:10
Pis	26	*08:50
Ari	28	*21:41
Tau	31	*10:28
Gem	2	*22:01
Can	5	*07:09
Leo	7	*12:57
Vir	9	*15:30
Lib	11	*15:47
Sco	13	*15:27
Sag	15	*16:23
Cap	17	*20:16

♈ Aries – Finding Your Moon Sign ☽

1950		
Tau	21	*08:32
Gem	23	*21:27
Can	26	*09:16
Leo	28	*18:04
Vir	30	*22:59
Lib	2	*00:39
Sco	4	*00:35
Sag	6	*00:37
Cap	8	*02:30
Aqu	10	*07:24
Pis	12	*15:38
Ari	15	*02:31
Tau	17	*14:59

1951		
Vir	21	*01:37
Lib	23	*07:20
Sco	25	*10:35
Sag	27	*12:40
Cap	29	*14:51
Aqu	31	*18:02
Pis	2	*22:45
Ari	5	*05:15
Tau	7	*13:52
Gem	10	*00:41
Can	12	*13:04
Leo	15	*01:17
Vir	17	*11:05
Lib	19	*17:13

1952		
Aqu	21	*07:54
Pis	23	*09:38
Ari	25	*11:34
Tau	27	*15:06
Gem	29	*21:36
Can	1	*07:39
Leo	3	*20:09
Vir	6	*08:39
Lib	8	*18:55
Sco	11	*02:12
Sag	13	*07:07
Cap	15	*10:41
Aqu	17	*13:43
Pis	19	*16:40

1953		
Can	22	*05:29
Leo	24	*16:14
Vir	27	*05:03
Lib	29	*17:51
Sco	1	*05:19
Sag	3	*14:57
Cap	5	*22:28
Aqu	8	*03:26
Pis	10	*05:49
Ari	12	*06:18
Tau	14	*06:31
Gem	16	*08:27
Can	18	*13:54

1954		
Sco	22	*04:26
Sag	24	*16:55
Cap	27	*03:54
Aqu	29	*11:35
Pis	31	*15:15
Ari	2	*15:39
Tau	4	*14:42
Gem	6	*14:40
Can	8	*17:28
Leo	11	*00:06
Vir	13	*10:03
Lib	15	*21:57
Sco	18	*10:32

♈ Aries – Finding Your Moon Sign ☽

1955			1956			1957			1958			1959		
Pis	21	*19:44	Leo	21	*21:30	Sag	20	*15:54	Ari	20	*11:17	Leo	20	*07:21
Ari	23	*23:08	Vir	23	*23:53	Cap	23	*00:35	Tau	23	*00:15	Vir	22	*12:26
Tau	26	*00:31	Lib	26	*03:00	Aqu	25	*12:17	Gem	25	*12:18	Lib	24	*14:26
Gem	28	*01:42	Sco	28	*08:19	Pis	28	*00:59	Can	27	*21:51	Sco	26	*14:53
Can	30	*04:05	Sag	30	*16:55	Ari	30	*12:54	Leo	30	*03:44	Sag	28	*15:31
Leo	1	*08:20	Cap	2	*04:37	Tau	1	*23:10	Vir	1	*06:00	Cap	30	*17:48
Vir	3	*14:31	Aqu	4	*17:24	Gem	4	*07:29	Lib	3	*05:53	Aqu	1	*22:42
Lib	5	*22:34	Pis	7	*04:36	Can	6	*13:36	Sco	5	*05:16	Pis	4	*06:23
Sco	8	*08:38	Ari	9	*12:45	Leo	8	*17:23	Sag	7	*06:06	Ari	6	*16:32
Sag	10	*20:41	Tau	11	*18:03	Vir	10	*19:12	Cap	9	*10:01	Tau	9	*04:31
Cap	13	*09:40	Gem	13	*21:30	Lib	12	*20:08	Aqu	11	*17:41	Gem	11	*17:24
Aqu	15	*21:18	Can	16	*00:14	Sco	14	*21:46	Pis	14	*04:38	Can	14	*05:47
Pis	18	*05:27	Leo	18	*03:00	Sag	17	*01:43	Ari	16	*17:22	Leo	16	*15:54
						Cap	19	*09:08	Tau	19	*06:16	Vir	18	*22:26

♈ Aries – Finding Your Moon Sign ☽

1960		
Cap	20	*07:14
Aqu	22	*10:10
Pis	24	*14:02
Ari	26	*19:29
Tau	29	*03:13
Gem	31	*13:32
Can	3	*01:45
Leo	5	*14:00
Vir	8	*00:00
Lib	10	*06:35
Sco	12	*10:00
Sag	14	*11:37
Cap	16	*13:01
Aqu	18	*15:32

1961		
Gem	21	*10:33
Can	23	*20:22
Leo	26	*08:48
Vir	28	*21:29
Lib	31	*08:20
Sco	2	*16:36
Sag	4	*22:33
Cap	7	*02:51
Aqu	9	*06:02
Pis	11	*08:31
Ari	13	*10:55
Tau	15	*14:17
Gem	17	*19:55

1962		
Lib	21	*07:28
Sco	23	*19:28
Sag	26	*05:48
Cap	28	*13:44
Aqu	30	*18:42
Pis	1	*20:41
Ari	3	*20:40
Tau	5	*20:25
Gem	7	*22:00
Can	10	*03:13
Leo	12	*12:36
Vir	15	*00:56
Lib	17	*13:53

1963		
Aqu	21	*01:19
Pis	23	*05:03
Ari	25	*05:37
Tau	27	*04:56
Gem	29	*05:13
Can	31	*08:14
Leo	2	*14:46
Vir	5	*00:20
Lib	7	*11:49
Sco	10	*00:13
Sag	12	*12:47
Cap	15	*00:26
Aqu	17	*09:32
Pis	19	*14:52

1964		
Can	20	*20:11
Leo	23	*00:15
Vir	25	*05:41
Lib	27	*12:48
Sco	29	*22:04
Sag	1	*09:40
Cap	3	*22:35
Aqu	6	*10:23
Pis	8	*18:46
Ari	10	*23:07
Tau	13	*00:36
Gem	15	*01:06
Can	17	*02:24
Leo	19	*05:39

♈ Aries – Finding Your Moon Sign ☽

1965		
Sag	22	*05:36
Cap	24	*17:06
Aqu	27	*05:58
Pis	29	*17:31
Ari	1	*02:17
Tau	3	*08:28
Gem	5	*12:54
Can	7	*16:24
Leo	9	*19:23
Vir	11	*22:14
Lib	14	*01:38
Sco	16	*06:42
Sag	18	*14:32

1966		
Ari	22	*02:32
Tau	24	*13:31
Gem	26	*22:40
Can	29	*05:23
Leo	31	*09:11
Vir	2	*10:30
Lib	4	*10:39
Sco	6	*11:30
Sag	8	*14:54
Cap	10	*22:02
Aqu	13	*08:42
Pis	15	*21:13
Ari	18	*09:26

1967		
Leo	21	*18:03
Vir	23	*20:07
Lib	25	*19:49
Sco	27	*19:10
Sag	29	*20:08
Cap	1	*00:11
Aqu	3	*07:49
Pis	5	*18:28
Ari	8	*06:56
Tau	10	*19:55
Gem	13	*08:14
Can	15	*18:36
Leo	18	*01:52

1968		
Cap	21	*09:35
Aqu	23	*14:17
Pis	25	*21:15
Ari	28	*06:31
Tau	30	*17:54
Gem	2	*06:40
Can	4	*19:12
Leo	7	*05:28
Vir	9	*12:02
Lib	11	*14:59
Sco	13	*15:31
Sag	15	*15:23
Cap	17	*16:23
Aqu	19	*19:57

1969		
Tau	20	*16:20
Gem	23	*02:13
Can	25	*14:18
Leo	28	*02:36
Vir	30	*12:52
Lib	1	*20:02
Sco	4	*00:21
Sag	6	*02:57
Cap	8	*05:04
Aqu	10	*07:46
Pis	12	*11:41
Ari	14	*17:13
Tau	17	*00:43
Gem	19	*10:28

♈ Aries – Finding Your Moon Sign ☽

1970

Vir	20	*10:29
Lib	22	*21:55
Sco	25	*07:09
Sag	27	*14:05
Cap	29	*18:59
Aqu	31	*22:07
Pis	3	*00:00
Ari	5	*01:31
Tau	7	*04:02
Gem	9	*09:02
Can	11	*17:33
Leo	14	*05:15
Lib	19	*05:34

1971

Cap	20	*04:36
Aqu	22	*09:27
Pis	24	*11:06
Ari	26	*10:45
Tau	28	*10:16
Gem	30	*11:44
Can	1	*16:51
Leo	4	*02:06
Vir	6	*14:16
Lib	9	*03:16
Sco	11	*15:27
Sag	14	*02:02
Cap	16	*10:37
Aqu	18	*16:45

1972

Can	21	*23:27
Leo	24	*05:45
Vir	26	*14:48
Lib	29	*01:42
Sco	31	*13:48
Sag	3	*02:26
Cap	5	*14:19
Aqu	7	*23:35
Pis	10	*04:57
Ari	12	*06:32
Tau	14	*05:54
Gem	16	*05:16
Can	18	*06:46

1973

Sco	21	*11:16
Sag	23	*22:26
Cap	26	*11:15
Aqu	28	*23:11
Pis	31	*07:54
Ari	2	*12:46
Tau	4	*14:57
Gem	6	*16:11
Can	8	*18:04
Leo	10	*21:31
Vir	13	*02:47
Lib	15	*09:50
Sco	17	*18:51

1974

Pis	21	*06:33
Ari	23	*16:01
Tau	25	*23:08
Gem	28	*04:32
Can	30	*08:39
Leo	1	*11:40
Vir	3	*13:56
Lib	5	*16:22
Sco	7	*20:25
Sag	10	*03:27
Cap	12	*13:56
Aqu	15	*02:33
Pis	17	*14:43

♈ Aries — Finding Your Moon Sign ☽

1975		
Can	20	*20:47
Leo	23	*00:29
Vir	25	*01:20
Lib	27	*00:51
Sco	29	*01:08
Sag	31	*04:10
Cap	2	*11:09
Aqu	4	*21:45
Pis	7	*10:16
Ari	9	*22:43
Tau	12	*09:52
Gem	14	*19:13
Can	17	*02:26
Leo	19	*07:13

1976		
Sag	20	*10:34
Cap	22	*14:49
Aqu	24	*22:20
Pis	27	*08:34
Ari	29	*20:37
Tau	1	*09:33
Gem	3	*22:14
Can	6	*09:05
Leo	8	*16:35
Vir	10	*20:14
Lib	12	*20:53
Sco	14	*20:14
Sag	16	*20:15
Cap	18	*22:44

1977		
Tau	22	*07:05
Gem	24	*19:38
Can	27	*08:16
Leo	29	*18:40
Vir	1	*01:23
Lib	3	*04:38
Sco	5	*05:39
Sag	7	*06:08
Cap	9	*07:40
Aqu	11	*11:24
Pis	13	*17:49
Ari	16	*02:52
Tau	18	*14:02

1978		
Vir	22	*01:48
Lib	24	*09:40
Sco	26	*15:00
Sag	28	*18:37
Cap	30	*21:23
Aqu	2	*00:05
Pis	4	*03:20
Ari	6	*07:51
Tau	8	*14:22
Gem	10	*23:28
Can	13	*10:59
Leo	15	*23:29
Vir	18	*10:42

1979		
Cap	21	*10:55
Aqu	23	*13:51
Pis	25	*15:04
Ari	27	*15:47
Tau	29	*17:36
Gem	31	*22:09
Can	3	*06:23
Leo	5	*17:57
Vir	8	*06:51
Lib	10	*18:44
Sco	13	*04:15
Sag	15	*11:17
Cap	17	*16:22
Aqu	19	*20:01

♈ Aries – Finding Your Moon Sign ☽

1980		
Gem	21	*01:48
Can	23	*06:55
Leo	25	*15:58
Vir	28	*03:52
Lib	30	*16:48
Sco	2	*05:21
Sag	4	*16:34
Cap	7	*01:41
Aqu	9	*07:58
Pis	11	*11:05
Ari	13	*11:39
Tau	15	*11:11
Gem	17	*11:42
Can	19	*15:12

1981		
Lib	20	*15:30
Sco	23	*03:14
Sag	25	*15:50
Cap	28	*03:51
Aqu	30	*13:14
Pis	1	*18:40
Ari	3	*20:24
Tau	5	*20:04
Gem	7	*19:47
Can	9	*21:34
Leo	12	*02:37
Vir	14	*10:57
Lib	16	*21:38
Sco	19	*09:38

1982		
Aqu	20	*11:51
Pis	22	*21:00
Ari	25	*02:36
Tau	27	*05:39
Gem	29	*07:43
Can	31	*10:09
Leo	2	*13:36
Vir	4	*18:18
Lib	7	*00:27
Sco	9	*08:33
Sag	11	*19:06
Cap	14	*07:41
Aqu	16	*20:17
Pis	19	*06:19

1983		
Can	22	*00:51
Leo	24	*03:42
Vir	26	*05:17
Lib	28	*06:48
Sco	30	*09:57
Sag	1	*16:20
Cap	4	*02:30
Aqu	6	*15:06
Pis	9	*03:29
Ari	11	*13:36
Tau	13	*20:58
Gem	16	*02:14
Can	18	*06:13

1984		
Sag	21	*17:41
Cap	24	*00:37
Aqu	26	*11:09
Pis	28	*23:37
Ari	31	*12:13
Tau	2	*23:54
Gem	5	*10:03
Can	7	*17:59
Leo	9	*23:00
Vir	12	*01:10
Lib	14	*01:29
Sco	16	*01:41
Sag	18	*03:44

♈ Aries – Finding Your Moon Sign ☽

1985		
Ari	21	*10:20
Tau	23	*23:06
Gem	26	*12:01
Can	28	*23:12
Leo	31	*06:51
Vir	2	*10:23
Lib	4	*10:53
Sco	6	*10:10
Sag	8	*10:18
Cap	10	*12:58
Aqu	12	*19:04
Pis	15	*04:30
Ari	17	*16:18

1986		
Leo	21	*07:37
Vir	23	*14:38
Lib	25	*18:22
Sco	27	*20:05
Sag	29	*21:20
Cap	31	*23:25
Aqu	3	*03:11
Pis	5	*09:04
Ari	7	*17:12
Tau	10	*03:36
Gem	12	*15:50
Can	15	*04:41
Leo	17	*16:09

1987		
Sag	20	*10:31
Cap	22	*13:48
Aqu	24	*16:18
Pis	26	*18:45
Ari	28	*22:12
Tau	31	*03:46
Gem	2	*12:17
Can	4	*23:33
Leo	7	*12:03
Vir	9	*23:27
Lib	12	*08:04
Sco	14	*13:39
Sag	16	*17:01
Cap	18	*19:20

1988		
Tau	20	*07:05
Gem	22	*11:22
Can	24	*19:27
Leo	27	*06:53
Vir	29	*19:48
Lib	1	*08:04
Sco	3	*18:25
Sag	6	*02:28
Cap	8	*08:18
Aqu	10	*12:09
Pis	12	*14:23
Ari	14	*15:46
Tau	16	*17:31
Gem	18	*21:10

1989		
Lib	22	*06:23
Sco	24	*19:10
Sag	27	*06:53
Cap	29	*16:24
Aqu	31	*22:43
Pis	3	*01:35
Ari	5	*01:50
Tau	7	*01:07
Gem	9	*01:32
Can	11	*04:58
Leo	13	*12:32
Vir	15	*23:39
Lib	18	*12:31

♈ Aries – Finding Your Moon Sign ☽

1990		
Cap	19	*17:01
Aqu	22	*02:29
Pis	24	*08:07
Ari	26	*10:14
Tau	28	*10:26
Gem	30	*10:42
Can	1	*12:50
Leo	3	*17:49
Vir	6	*01:42
Lib	8	*11:44
Sco	10	*23:17
Sag	13	*11:47
Cap	16	*00:14
Aqu	18	*10:51

1991		
Gem	20	*23:36
Can	23	*02:27
Leo	25	*05:43
Vir	27	*09:41
Lib	29	*14:49
Sco	31	*22:01
Sag	3	*07:59
Cap	5	*20:19
Aqu	8	*08:58
Pis	10	*19:17
Ari	13	*01:48
Tau	15	*05:05
Gem	17	*06:41
Can	19	*08:17

1992		
Sco	20	*23:21
Sag	23	*05:13
Cap	25	*15:09
Aqu	28	*03:44
Pis	30	*16:22
Ari	2	*03:03
Tau	4	*11:17
Gem	6	*17:32
Can	8	*22:17
Leo	11	*01:45
Vir	13	*04:08
Lib	15	*06:10
Sco	17	*09:10
Sag	19	*14:41

1993		
Pis	20	*13:10
Ari	23	*01:51
Tau	25	*13:58
Gem	28	*00:47
Can	30	*09:13
Leo	1	*14:20
Vir	3	*16:09
Lib	5	*15:54
Sco	7	*15:32
Sag	9	*17:09
Cap	11	*22:25
Aqu	14	*07:36
Pis	16	*19:32
Ari	19	*08:14

1994		
Can	20	*12:52
Leo	22	*20:37
Vir	25	*00:12
Lib	27	*00:45
Sco	29	*00:15
Sag	31	*00:42
Cap	2	*03:38
Aqu	4	*09:46
Pis	6	*18:51
Ari	9	*06:08
Tau	11	*18:47
Gem	14	*07:47
Can	16	*19:40
Leo	19	*04:44

♈ Aries – Finding Your Moon Sign ☽

1995			1996			1997			1998			1999			2000		
Sag	21	*12:57	Tau	21	*16:58	Vir	21	*08:59	Cap	21	*06:43	Tau	20	*01:08	Lib	20	*04:57
Cap	23	*15:31	Gem	24	*01:00	Lib	23	*21:34	Aqu	23	*13:00	Gem	22	*02:05	Sco	22	*11:18
Aqu	25	*19:09	Can	26	*12:06	Sco	26	*08:41	Pis	25	*15:41	Can	24	*04:33	Sag	24	*20:43
Pis	28	*00:18	Leo	29	*00:36	Sag	28	*17:39	Ari	27	*15:48	Leo	26	*09:22	Cap	27	*08:50
Ari	30	*07:25	Vir	31	*12:13	Cap	31	*00:05	Tau	29	*15:06	Vir	28	*16:34	Aqu	29	*21:33
Tau	1	*16:58	Lib	2	*21:25	Aqu	2	*03:58	Gem	31	*15:38	Lib	31	*01:49	Pis	1	*08:11
Gem	4	*04:49	Sco	5	*03:56	Pis	4	*05:41	Can	2	*19:09	Sco	2	*12:48	Ari	3	*15:20
Can	6	*17:39	Sag	7	*08:21	Ari	6	*06:18	Leo	5	*02:36	Sag	5	*01:07	Tau	5	*19:28
Leo	9	*05:15	Cap	9	*11:29	Tau	8	*07:20	Vir	7	*13:25	Cap	7	*13:38	Gem	7	*21:58
Vir	11	*13:37	Aqu	11	*14:09	Gem	10	*10:29	Lib	10	*02:04	Aqu	10	*00:23	Can	10	*00:16
Lib	13	*18:19	Pis	13	*16:59	Can	12	*17:03	Sco	12	*14:55	Pis	12	*07:33	Leo	12	*03:16
Sco	15	*20:12	Ari	15	*20:42	Leo	15	*03:22	Sag	15	*02:51	Ari	14	*10:44	Vir	14	*07:18
Sag	17	*20:51	Tau	18	*02:06	Vir	17	*16:00	Cap	17	*13:04	Tau	16	*11:06	Lib	16	*12:36
Cap	19	*21:54							Aqu	19	*20:40	Gem	18	*10:39	Sco	18	*19:35

♈ Aries Mercury Signs ☿

YEAR	PISCES	ARIES	TAURUS
1930	20 Mar–26 Mar	26 Mar–10 Apr	10 Apr–21 Apr
1931		21 Mar–3 Apr	3 Apr–19 Apr
1932		20 Mar–20 Apr	
1933	25 Mar–17 Apr	21 Mar–25 Mar	
		17 Apr–20 Apr	
1934	21 Mar–15 Apr	15 Apr–20 Apr	
1935	21 Mar–8 Apr	8 Apr–21 Apr	
1936	20 Mar–31 Mar	31 Mar–15 Apr	15 Apr–20 Apr
1937	21 Mar–23 Mar	23 Mar–7 Apr	7 Apr–20 Apr
1938		21 Mar–1 Apr	1 Apr–20 Apr
1939		21 Mar–20 Apr	
1940	20 Mar–17 Apr	17 Apr–20 Apr	
1941	21 Mar–12 Apr	12 Apr–20 Apr	
1942	21 Mar–5 Apr	5 Apr–20 Apr	20 Apr
1943	21 Mar–28 Mar	28 Mar–12 Apr	12 Apr–20 Apr
1944		20 Mar–3 Apr	3 Apr–20 Apr
1945		20 Mar–20 Apr	
1946	1 Apr–16 Apr	21 Mar–1 Apr	
		16 Apr–20 Apr	
1947	21 Mar–16 Apr	16 Apr–20 Apr	
1948	20 Mar–9 Apr	9 Apr–20 Apr	
1949	20 Mar–1 Apr	1 Apr–16 Apr	16 Apr–20 Apr
1950	21 Mar–24 Mar	24 Mar–8 Apr	8 Apr–20 Apr
1951		20 Mar–2 Apr	2 Apr–20 Apr
1952		20 Mar–20 Apr	
1953	21 Mar–17 Apr	17 Apr–20 Apr	
1954	21 Mar–13 Apr	13 Apr–20 Apr	
1955	21 Mar–6 Apr	6 Apr–20 Apr	
1956	20 Mar–28 Mar	28 Mar–12 Apr	12 Apr–20 Apr

YEAR	PISCES	ARIES	TAURUS
1957		20 Mar–4 Apr	4 Apr–20 Apr
1958		21 Mar–2 Apr	2 Apr–10 Apr
		10 Apr–20 Apr	
1959		21 Mar–20 Apr	
1960	20 Mar–16 Apr	16 Apr–20 Apr	
1961	20 Mar–10 Apr	10 Apr–20 Apr	
1962	21 Mar–3 Apr	3 Apr–18 Apr	18 Apr–20 Apr
1963	21 Mar–26 Mar	26 Mar–9 Apr	9 Apr–20 Apr
1964		20 Mar–2 Apr	2 Apr–20 Apr
1965		20 Mar–20 Apr	
1966	22 Mar–17 Apr	21 Mar–22 Mar	
		17 Apr–20 Apr	
1967	21 Mar–14 Apr	14 Apr–20 Apr	
1968	20 Mar–7 Apr	7 Apr–20 Apr	
1969	20 Mar–30 Mar	30 Mar–14 Apr	14 Apr–20 Apr
1970	21 Mar–22 Mar	22 Mar–6 Apr	6 Apr–20 Apr
1971		21 Mar–1 Apr	1 Apr–18 Apr
		18 Apr–20 Apr	
1972		20 Mar–19 Apr	
1973	20 Mar–16 Apr	16 Apr–20 Apr	
1974	21 Mar–11 Apr	11 Apr–20 Apr	
1975	21 Mar–4 Apr	4 Apr–20 Apr	
1976	20 Mar–26 Mar	26 Mar–10 Apr	10 Apr–19 Apr
1977		20 Mar–3 Apr	3 Apr–20 Apr
1978		20 Mar–20 Apr	
1979	28 Mar–17 Apr	21 Mar–28 Mar	
		17 Apr–20 Apr	
1980	20 Mar–14 Apr	14 Apr–19 Apr	
1981	20 Mar–8 Apr	8 Apr–20 Apr	
1982	20 Mar–31 Mar	31 mar–15 Apr	15 Apr–20 Apr
1983	21 Mar–23 Mar	23 Mar–7 Apr	7 Apr–20 Apr
1984		20 Mar–31 Mar	31 Mar–19 Apr

YEAR	PISCES	ARIES	TAURUS
1985		20 Mar–20 Apr	
1986	20 Mar–17 Apr	17 Apr–20 Apr	
1987	21 Mar–12 Apr	12 Apr–20 Apr	
1988	20 Mar–4 Apr	4 Apr–20 Apr	20 Apr–21 Apr
1989	20 Mar–28 Mar	28 Mar–11 Apr	11 Apr–20 Apr
1990		20 Mar–4 Apr	4 Apr–20 Apr
1991		21 Mar–20 Apr	
1992	4 Apr–14 Apr	20 Mar–4 Apr	
		14 Apr–19 Apr	
1993	20 Mar–15 Apr	15 Apr–20 Apr	
1994	20 Mar–9 Apr	9 Apr–20 Apr	
1995	20 Mar–2 Apr	2 Apr–17 Apr	17 Apr–20 Apr
1996	20 Mar–24 Mar	24 Mar–8 Apr	8 Apr–19 Apr
1997		20 Mar–1 Apr	1 Apr–20 Apr
1998		20 Mar–20 Apr	
1999	21 Mar–17 Apr	17 Apr–20 Apr	
2000	20 Mar–13 Apr	13 Apr–19 Apr	

♈ Aries Venus Signs ♀

YEAR	AQUARIUS	PISCES	ARIES	TAURUS	GEMINI
1930			21 Mar–6 Apr	6 Apr–20 Apr	
1931	21 Mar–31 Mar	31 Mar–21 Apr			
1932				20 Mar–5 Apr	5 Apr–21 Apr
1933				21 Mar–27 Mar	27 Mar–20 Apr
1934	21 Mar–6 Apr	6 Apr–20 Apr			
1935			21 Mar–22 Mar	22 Mar–16 Apr	16 Apr–21 Apr
1936		20 Mar–11 Apr	11 Apr–20 Apr		
1937			14 Apr–20 Apr	20 Mar–14 Apr	
1938			21 Mar–5 Apr	5 Apr–20 Apr	
1939	21 Mar–31 Mar	31 Mar–20 Apr			
1940				20 Mar–4 Apr	4 Apr–20 Apr
1941		21 Mar–27 Mar	27 Mar–20 Apr	20 Apr	
1942	21 Mar–6 Apr	6 Apr–20 Apr			
1943			21 Mar	21 Mar–15 Apr	15 Apr–20 Apr
1944		20 Mar–10 Apr	10 Apr–20 Apr		

YEAR	AQUARIUS	PISCES	ARIES	TAURUS	GEMINI
1945			7 Apr–20 Apr	20 Mar–7 Apr	
1946			21 Mar–5 Apr	5 Apr–20 Apr	
1947	21 Mar–30 Mar	30 Mar–20 Apr			
1948			26 Mar–20 Apr	20 Mar–4 Apr	4 Apr–20 Apr
1949		20 Mar–26 Mar			
1950	21 Mar–6 Apr	6 Apr–20 Apr			
1951			21 Mar	21 Mar–15 Apr	15 Apr–20 Apr
1952		20 Mar–31 Mar	31 Mar–20 Apr		
1953			31 Mar–20 Apr	20 Mar–31 Mar	
1954			21 Mar–4 Apr	4 Apr–20 Apr	
1955	21 Mar–4 Apr	4 Apr–20 Apr			
1956				20 Mar–4 Apr	4 Apr–20 Apr
1957		20 Mar–25 Mar	25 Mar–19 Apr	19 Apr–20 Apr	
1958	21 Mar–6 Apr	6 Apr–20 Apr			
1959				21 Mar–14 Apr	14 Apr–20 Apr
1960		20 Mar–9 Apr	9 Apr–20 Apr		
1961			20 Mar–20 Apr		
1962			21 Mar–3 Apr	3 Apr–20 Apr	
1963	21 Mar–30 Mar	30 Mar–20 Apr			

YEAR	AQUARIUS	PISCES	ARIES	TAURUS	GEMINI
1964		20 Mar–25 Mar	25 Mar–18 Apr	20 Mar–4 Apr	4 Apr–20 Apr
1965		6 Apr–20 Apr		18 Apr–20 Apr	
1966	21 Mar–6 Apr				
1967		21 Mar–14 Apr	14 Apr–20 Apr		
1968		20 Mar–8 Apr	8 Apr–20 Apr		
1969			20 Mar–20 Apr		
1970			21 Mar–3 Apr	3 Apr–20 Apr	
1971	21 Mar–29 Mar	29 Mar–20 Apr			
1972				20 Mar–3 Apr	3 Apr–20 Apr
1973		20 Mar–24 Mar	24 Mar–18 Apr	18 Apr–20 Apr	
1974	21 Mar–6 Apr	6 Apr–20 Apr			
1975				21 Mar–13 Apr	13 Apr–20 Apr
1976		20 Mar–8 Apr	8 Apr–20 Apr		
1977			20 Mar–20 Apr		
1978			20 Mar–2 Apr	2 Apr–20 Apr	
1979	21 Mar–29 Mar	29 Mar– 20 Apr			
1980			20 Mar–3 Apr	3 Apr–20 Apr	
1981		20 Mar–24 Mar	24 Mar–17 Apr	17 Apr–20 Apr	
1982	20 Mar–6 Apr	6 Apr–20 Apr			

YEAR	AQUARIUS	PISCES	ARIES	TAURUS	GEMINI
1983				21 Mar–13 Apr	13 Apr–20 Apr
1984		20 Mar–7 Apr	7 Apr–20 Apr		
1985			20 Mar–20 Apr		
1986	21 Mar–28 Mar		20 Mar–2 Apr	2 Apr–20 Apr	
1987		28 Mar–20 Apr			3 Apr–20 Apr
1988				20 Mar–3 Apr	
1989		20 Mar–23 Mar	23 Mar–16 Apr	16 Apr–20 Apr	
1990	20 Mar–6 Apr	6 Apr–20 Apr			
1991				21 Mar–13 Apr	13 Apr–20 Apr
1992		20 Mar–7 Apr	7 Apr–20 Apr		
1993			20 Mar–20 Apr		
1994			20 Mar–1 Apr	1 Apr–20 Apr	
1995	21 Mar–28 Mar	28 Mar–20 Apr			
1996				20 Mar–3 Apr	3 Apr–20 Apr
1997		20 Mar–23 Mar	23 Mar–16 Apr	16 Apr–20 Apr	
1998	20 Mar–6 Apr	6 Apr–20 Apr			
1999				21 Mar–12 Apr	12 Apr–20 Apr
2000		21 Mar–6 Apr	6 Apr–20 Apr		

The Aries Workbook

There are no right or wrong answers in this chapter. Its aim is to help you assess how you are doing with your life – in YOUR estimation – and to make the material of this book more personal and, I hope, more helpful for you.

1.The Aries in You
Which of the following Aries characteristics do you recognise in yourself?

daring	assertive	hot-blooded
exuberant	direct	independent
spontaneous	energetic	competitive
heroic	pioneering	courageous

2. In which situations do you find yourself acting like this?

_____

_____

3. When you are feeling vulnerable, you may show some of the less constructive Aries traits. Do you recognise yourself in any of the following?

irresponsible	aggressive	selfish
bossy	impatient	pushy
naive	bad-tempered	abrasive

What kind of situations trigger off this behaviour and what do you think might help you, in these situations, to respond more positively?

_____
_____

4. You and Your Roles

a) Where, if anywhere, in your life do you play the role of Hero?

_____
_____

b) Who, or what, do you challenge?

_____
_____

5. Do you play any of the following roles – in the literal or broad sense – in any part of your life? If not, would you like to? What might be your first step towards doing so?

Warrior	Pioneer	Daredevil
Competitor	Hunter	Leader

_____
_____

6. Sun Aspects

If any of the following planets aspects your Sun, add each of the keywords for that planet to complete the following sentences. Which phrases ring true for you?

I am _____

My father is _____

My job requires that I am _____

Saturn Words (Use only if your Sun is aspected by Saturn)

ambitious	controlling	judgmental	mature
serious	strict	traditional	bureaucratic
cautious	committed	hard-working	disciplined
depressive	responsible	status-seeking	limiting

Uranus Words (Use only if your Sun is aspected by Uranus)

freedom-loving	progressive	rebellious	shocking
scientific	cutting-edge	detached	contrary
friendly	disruptive	eccentric	humanitarian
innovative	nonconformist	unconventional	exciting

Neptune Words (Use only if your Sun is aspected by Neptune)

sensitive	idealistic	artistic	impressionable
disappointing	impractical	escapist	self-sacrificing
spiritual	unrealistic	dreamy	glamorous
dependent	deceptive	rescuing	blissful

Pluto Words (Use only if your Sun is aspected by Pluto)

powerful	single-minded	intense	extreme
secretive	rotten	passionate	mysterious
investigative	uncompromising	ruthless	wealthy
abusive	regenerative	associated with sex, birth or death	

a) If one or more negative words describe you or your job, how might you turn that quality into something more positive or satisfying?

_____

_____

7. The Moon and You

Below are brief lists of what the Moon needs, in the various elements, to feel secure and satisfied. First find your Moon element, then estimate how much of each of the following you are expressing and receiving in your life, especially at home and in your relationships, on a scale of 0 to 5 where 0 = none and 5 = plenty.

FIRE MOONS — Aries, Leo, Sagittarius

attention	action	drama
recognition	self-expression	spontaneity
enthusiasm	adventure	leadership

EARTH MOONS — Taurus, Virgo, Capricorn

stability	orderly routine	sensual pleasures
material security	a sense of rootedness	control over your home life
regular body care	practical achievements	pleasurable practical tasks

AIR MOONS — Gemini, Libra, Aquarius

mental rapport	stimulating ideas	emotional space
friendship	social justice	interesting conversations
fairness	socialising	freedom to circulate

WATER MOONS — Cancer, Scorpio, Pisces

intimacy	a sense of belonging	emotional rapport
emotional safety	respect for your feelings	time and space to retreat
acceptance	cherishing and being cherished	warmth and comfort

a) Do you feel your Moon is being 'fed' enough?

yes _____ no _____

b) How might you satisfy your Moon needs even better?

_____

_____

8. You and Your Mercury

As an Aries, your Mercury can only be in Pisces, Aries or Taurus. Below are some of the ways and situations in which Mercury in each of the elements might learn and communicate effectively. First find your Mercury sign, then circle the words you think apply to you.

Mercury in Fire (Aries)

action	imagination	identifying with the subject matter
excitement	drama	playing with possibilities

Mercury in Earth (Taurus)

time-tested methods	useful facts	well-structured information
'how to' instructions	demonstrations	hands-on experience

Mercury in Air (As an Aries, you can never have Mercury in an air sign; the words are included here for completeness)

facts arranged in categories	logic	demonstrable connections
rational arguments	theories	debate and sharing of ideas

Mercury in Water (Pisces)

pictures and images	charged atmospheres	feeling-linked information
intuitive understanding	emotional rapport	being shown personally

a) This game with Mercury can be done with a friend or on your own. Skim through a magazine until you find a picture that interests you. Then describe the picture – to your friend, or in writing or on tape. Notice what you emphasise and the kind of words you use. Now try to describe it using the language and emphasis of each of the other Mercury modes. How easy did you find that? Identifying the preferred Mercury style of others and using that style yourself can lead to improved communication all round.

9. Your Venus Values

Below are lists of qualities and situations that your Venus sign might enjoy. Assess on a scale of 0 to 5 how much your Venus desires and pleasures are met and expressed in your life. 0 = not at all, 5 = fully.

Venus in Aries

You will activate your Venus by taking part in anything that makes you feel potent, for example:

taking the initiative	competition	risk-taking
action dramas	taking the lead	tough challenges

Venus in Taurus

You will activate your Venus through whatever pleases the senses and enhances your sense of stability, for example:

financial security	beauty	gardening and nature
sensual pleasures	good food	body pampering

Venus in Gemini

You will activate your Venus through anything that stimulates your mind and uses a talent for making connections, for example:

playing go-between	flirting	talking and writing
passing on new ideas	witty use of words	trend-spotting

Venus in Aquarius
You will activate your Venus through freedom from the restraints of convention, for example:

sharing progressive ideas	unusual relationships	being nonconformist
humanitarian projects	teamwork	eccentric fashions

Venus in Pisces
You will activate your Venus through anything that allows you to experience fusion with something greater than yourself, for example:

relieving suffering	daydreaming	creating a glamorous image
spiritual devotion	voluntary service	losing yourself in art, music or love

a) How, and where, might you have more fun and pleasure by bringing more of what your Venus sign loves into your life?

_____

_____

b) Make a note here of the kind of gifts your Venus sign would love to receive. Then go on and spoil yourself . . .

_____

_____

Resources

Finding an Astrologer

I'm often asked what is the best way to find a reputable astrologer. Personal recommendation by someone whose judgement you trust is by far the best way. Ideally, the astrologer should also be endorsed by a reputable organisation whose members adhere to a strict code of ethics, which guarantees confidentiality and professional conduct.

Contact Addresses

Association of Professional Astrologers
www.professionalastrologers.org

APA members adhere to a strict code of professional ethics.

Astrological Association of Great Britain
www.astrologicalassociation.co.uk

The main body for astrology in the UK that also has information on astrological events and organisations throughout the world.

Faculty of Astrological Studies
www.astrology.org.uk

The teaching body internationally recognised for excellence in astrological education at all levels.

Your Aries Friends

You can keep a record of Ariens you know here, with the page numbers of where to find their descriptions handy for future reference.

Name _____ Date of Birth _____

Aspects★	None	Saturn	Uranus	Neptune	Pluto
Moon Sign _____				p _____	
Mercury Sign _____				p _____	
Venus Sign _____				p _____	

Name _____ Date of Birth _____

Aspects★	None	Saturn	Uranus	Neptune	Pluto
Moon Sign _____				p _____	
Mercury Sign _____				p _____	
Venus Sign _____				p _____	

Name _____ Date of Birth _____

Aspects★	None	Saturn	Uranus	Neptune	Pluto
Moon Sign _____				p _____	
Mercury Sign _____				p _____	
Venus Sign _____				p _____	

Name _____ Date of Birth _____

Aspects★	None	Saturn	Uranus	Neptune	Pluto
Moon Sign _____				p _____	
Mercury Sign _____				p _____	
Venus Sign _____				p _____	

★ Circle where applicable

Sign Summaries

SIGN	GLYPH	APPROX DATES	SYMBOL	ROLE	ELEMENT	QUALITY	PLANET	GLYPH	KEYWORD
1. Aries	♈	21/3 – 19/4	Ram	Hero	Fire	Cardinal	Mars	♂	Assertiveness
2. Taurus	♉	20/4 – 20/5	Bull	Steward	Earth	Fixed	Venus	♀	Stability
3. Gemini	♊	21/5 – 21/6	Twins	Go-Between	Air	Mutable	Mercury	☿	Communication
4. Cancer	♋	22/6 – 22/7	Crab	Caretaker	Water	Cardinal	Moon	☽	Nurture
5. Leo	♌	23/7 – 22/8	Lion	Performer	Fire	Fixed	Sun	☉	Glory
6. Virgo	♍	23/8 – 22/9	Maiden	Craftworker	Earth	Mutable	Mercury	☿	Skill
7. Libra	♎	23/9 – 22/10	Scales	Architect	Air	Cardinal	Venus	♀	Balance
8. Scorpio	♏	23/10 – 23/11	Scorpion	Survivor	Water	Fixed	Pluto	♇	Transformation
9. Sagittarius	♐	22/11 – 21/12	Archer	Adventurer	Fire	Mutable	Jupiter	♃	Wisdom
10. Capricorn	♑	22/12 – 19/1	Goat	Manager	Earth	Cardinal	Saturn	♄	Responsibility
11. Aquarius	♒	20/1 – 19/2	Waterbearer	Scientist	Air	Fixed	Uranus	♅	Progress
12. Pisces	♓	20/2 – 20/3	Fishes	Dreamer	Water	Mutable	Neptune	♆	Universality